"*We all win from diversity. Risha ..... makes it easy with her astonishing stories, inspiring conversations, and constant faith in our collective ability to come together and belong to one another. You can find the unexpected on every page because Risha doesn't miss a moment to teach us all how to 'do diversity right.' Be Better Than Your BS will change you, and you'll love it.*"

— **Dr. Marshall Goldsmith**, Thinkers50 award-winning executive coach and *New York Times* best-selling author of *The Earned Life*, *Triggers* and *What Got You Here Won't Get You There*

"*Risha's powerful message about intentionally engaging with people not like you is one I personally needed in my own life. The practical tips she shares in this book on how to do that will make the world a better place for us all to live and work in.*"

— **Rory Vaden**, co-founder of Brand Builders Group and *New York Times* best-selling author of *Take the Stairs*

"*I've always believed that leadership is about continuously improving oneself and inspiring others to do the same. Be Better Than Your BS is a powerful guidebook for anyone who wants to embrace this philosophy and become a better leader, a better teammate, and a better human being. Risha Grant's no-nonsense approach, practical advice, and inspiring stories will challenge you to confront your biases, expand your perspective, and take action toward positive change. This book is a must-read for anyone who wants to create a more inclusive, equitable, and successful workplace.*"

— **Captain Sandy Yawn**, author of *Be the Calm or Be the Storm* and star of Bravo's *Below Deck Mediterranean*

"*So real. So insightful. Risha openly shares her experiences and connects the dots to DEI initiatives that support companies dealing with experiences and challenges that cause disconnection within our cultures. Reading it reminded me of what I forgot or let become normal. I wish we had this book as a resource when we started our DEI journey.*"

— **Michelle Manglal-lan**, senior manager, Diversity, Equity & Inclusion, North America Region, Samsung Electronics America, Inc.

"*Risha Grant elevates and addresses the pain points many of our companies are experiencing in today's workplace. This book is a succinct and highly practical guide to building a culture of inclusion. I highly recommend it for leaders who want to take their company culture from disconnection to intentional engagement.*"

— **Anton Gunn**, best-selling author and
former advisor to Barack Obama

"*Your company culture dictates your work environment. Need to build trust among your teams? Want your employees to be aware of their unconscious biases? Want your leadership to build policies and systems that support a culture of inclusion?* Be Better Than Your BS *is the book to guide you to a culture where everyone thrives and belongs.*"

— **Stefanie K. Johnson**, *Wall Street Journal*
best-selling author of *Inclusify*

"*Humans are a messy bunch—you included. When we can overcome our mess and create a team where everyone feels included, we can achieve things we didn't think possible at first. Risha Grant's plainspoken style and personal experiences provide an enlightening path to reflect on your own roots and learn to include others by accepting yourself.*"

— **David Burkus**, author of *Leading from Anywhere*

"Be Better Than Your BS *is a refreshing, bold, and clear-eyed look in the mirror—with author Risha Grant standing right there with you. Risha will have you rethinking bigotry, equity, bias, and more. She'll also have you laughing. She'll leave you convinced that the world she describes—where everyone belongs and everyone contributes—is within our communal grasp.*"

— **Dorie Clark**, *Wall Street Journal* best-selling author of *The Long Game* and Duke University Fuqua School of Business executive education faculty member

BE *Better* THAN YOUR BS

ALSO BY RISHA GRANT

That's B.S.: How Bias Synapse Disrupts Inclusive Cultures and the Power to Attract Diverse Markets

BE *Better* THAN YOUR BS

HOW RADICAL ACCEPTANCE EMPOWERS AUTHENTICITY AND CREATES A WORKPLACE CULTURE OF INCLUSION

RISHA GRANT

HAY HOUSE LLC

Carlsbad, California • New York City

London • Sydney • New Delhi

Published in the United States by: Hay House LLC: www.hayhouse
.com® • **Published in Australia by:** Hay House Australia Publishing Pty
Ltd: www.hayhouse.com.au • **Published in the United Kingdom by:**
Hay House UK Ltd: www.hayhouse.co.uk • **Published in India by:** Hay
House Publishers (India) Pty Ltd: www.hayhouse.co.in

Indexer: Jay Kreider
Cover design: the Book Designers
Interior design: Karim J. Garcia
Interior photos/illustrations: Courtesy of the author

**Cataloging-in-Publication Data is
on file at the Library of Congress**

Tradepaper ISBN: 978-1-4019-7784-9
E-book ISBN: 978-1-4019-6999-8
Audiobook ISBN: 978-1-4019-7000-0

10 9 8 7 6 5 4 3 2 1
1st edition, August 2023
2nd edition, August 2024

SUSTAINABLE
FORESTRY
INITIATIVE

Certified Chain of Custody
Promoting Sustainable Forestry

www.forests.org
SFI-01268

SFI label applies to the text stock

Printed in the United States of America

This product uses responsibly sourced papers and/or recycled materials.
For more information, see www.hayhouse.com.

*This book is dedicated to
my favorite niece and nephew.*

*Kambry and Koen, since you were born I've
always hoped that the work I do would make
this world a better and safer place for you to live,
grow, and accomplish your goals. I want y'all to
dream big, make good decisions, work hard, and
live your lives on your terms. I have no doubt
that you will do this because our village is there
to guide, support, fuss, protect,
and love you through it.*

*Along your way, you will encounter those who are
bullied, ridiculed, marginalized, not accepted, or are
in some way "othered." My prayer for you is that you
stand for them, be a voice for them, and give the
support you've received back a hundredfold to those
who don't have a village or who have been
pushed to the outskirts of our society.*

*Be kind, show love,
and be better than your BS!*

CONTENTS

INTRODUCTION

Clutching your travel bag close to your body so you don't clock a fellow passenger in the head, you inch your way down the narrow aisle until you can finally cram yourself into your ridiculously small airplane seat and get yourself ready for takeoff. iPad? Check. Neck pillow? Check. Earbuds? Check. Gum? Gum??? Whew, found it. You lean back against your headrest and take a big breath. You're comfortable, but you know it won't last. There's no such thing as an open airplane seat nowadays; the empty one next to you isn't going to stay that way. Trying not to make eye contact, you scan the long line of passengers still shuffling in your direction, gauging who might be the least offensive seatmate for the next five hours. That woman in the ugly sweater is a snorer, you're sure of it. The idiot with the piercings looks like a damn anarchist. He's probably high. Please, God, not the baby. Anything but a mom and baby. No, no, no, not the chick with all the hair, either. What the . . . who let that turbaned guy on the plane?

In my work, I regularly face business audiences packed with people who are 100 percent certain they don't carry unconscious bias. Then I ask them to remember the last time they were in an airplane waiting to find out who would be sitting next to them for the duration of their trip. The energy in the room changes. Some people wince or offer a sheepish smile. Some nod. A lot of them even burst out laughing, knowing they're busted. I can see the shift in their faces. Because we've all been there! Maybe it happened in an airplane, maybe in an elevator, but every one of us has sized up a stranger based on nothing more than their dress, hair, tattoos, weight, race, or other random superficial detail. They say it takes about seven seconds to make a first impression, but this thought exercise shows that it takes less than a millisecond to pass judgment.

Now, in the office, we're frequently not dealing with strangers, but with colleagues and partners that we see every day. You might think, even if I am a little biased against a few strangers, that doesn't affect the way I interact with people at work.

Really? Are you sure? Someone shares an idea, makes a complaint, or asks you for an opportunity—and you don't think the subconscious judgments you make about strangers who look, dress, or act a certain way is going to influence your response?

What if you're wrong? Remember, we're talking about your subconscious, which is full of BS. What if, in fact, your bias does affect the way you interact with people at work? And what if, aside from being unfair and unjust, your bias is causing you to miss out on the big ideas and exchanges that could benefit and grow your company? Wouldn't you want to know?

I speak to thousands of people per month about the existence, persistence, and evidence of bias in the workplace, and how eliminating it is not only a moral imperative but a financial one. And every time, after realizing they can't fix a problem they can't see, someone asks, "So what do I do now?"

You become better than your BS.

How? Through Radical Acceptance (RA). This is a common term in the wellness world, referring to the act of relinquishing the urge to control or avoid pain and acknowledging reality so you can instead focus on improving your future. Yet as useful as that type of RA surely is, that's not what this book will teach you to achieve. The Radical Acceptance I teach doesn't help you tolerate pain; it prevents you from causing it.

I'm Risha Grant: culture connector; diversity, equity, and inclusion (DEI) expert; and consultant. I'm also a small-town, Black, woman, bisexual, cussing, left-handed, former Division 1 athlete, and ex-preacher's wife. I am diversity personified. And for many years I did my best to hide it, thinking it was the only way for a person like me to succeed.

Over 20 years ago, I started the first diversity communications firm in my home state of Oklahoma, where 74 percent of the population is white (non-Hispanic or Latino).[1] Black, Indigenous, and People of Color (BIPOC) have to claw their way to the promised land here, and I was determined to make it. That meant I spent the early years of my career working as hard to conform to my predominantly white, male-led business environment as I did convincing CEOs that it was in their best interest for their organizations to become more inclusive and work with or appeal to diverse markets.

It didn't work. Even the few companies that publicly professed a commitment to diversity and inclusion, as it was called back then, didn't care enough to invest in company initiatives unless they were being sued. I couldn't get backers. Most of the people I approached in the beginning were well-known men in the business community whom

I had known for years. I even knew their families. Come to find out these men who I respected so much were more interested in sex with me than with company shares. I found a female backer who I thought "got it" because she asked me if she could invest. Then out of the blue, she pulled out. I had a strong suspicion that someone close to her told her that diversity work was a bad investment.

There were days I couldn't buy food, and I had my lights, gas, and cable cut off. There were times I didn't have change for the meters to park outside my office. I amassed thousands in parking tickets, and several boots were put on my tires when I couldn't pay them. I had hundreds of foreclosure notices from my mortgage company, and thousands of insufficient-fund bank overdrafts. But I kept going, trying to overcome people's biases, trying to make them care, trying to break through the lip service, knowing all the while any success I achieved was contingent on the soul-sapping effort I constantly made to look, speak, and be the way corporate America wanted me to.

In 2016, I decided I had to preserve my sanity. I was done. I physically closed my doors, moved into my home office, and dedicated myself full-time to my one remaining client. I also came out to the world beyond my close friends and family. I'm not just talking about my sexuality. I mean I came out freely as myself—cussin', country, Ebonics, and all. I started talking in my normal "Black" voice. I wore my hair exactly the way I wanted to. I thought my career was finished. More important, I was so burnt out I didn't care. I had to do more to pay the bills, so I focused on writing my first book about bias while simultaneously hiring a speaking manager. In the book and my social media posts, I wrote as the real me, not as Risha-trying-to-please-everyone me. To my surprise, instead of rejecting the real me, companies—led mostly by white dudes—started seeking me out for speaking engagements. It turned out that the radical step of accepting myself increased my sense of value and belonging in a world that previously didn't seem made for people like me. Confidence like that is attractive; people want to be around it. But there's something else. Radically accepting myself gave me the clarity to observe my own biases and rise above them, which allowed me to judge less, behave more inclusively, and radically accept others (super helpful when you're a diversity, equity, and inclusion specialist). And so, with authenticity and diversity as my superpower, I focused solely on speaking gigs and training people how to be better than their BS, using DEI as my lens and what I called Radical Acceptance as my tool kit. And guess what? It worked.

In 2018, the year Starbucks had to shut down its stores to offer a day of "anti-bias training"[2] to quell the national outrage that erupted after an employee called the cops on two Black men who'd been sitting at a table for less than ten minutes to wait for their business partner to discuss a real estate deal, I was giving companies straight, no-chaser talk about unconscious bias and the need to invest in diversity and inclusion to tens of thousands of people per year. By 2019, there was one constant I could count on: every time an entitled white woman called the cops on a Black person over a perceived slight, or there was a national story about a Black person getting killed or shot by law enforcement, my phone would ring.

That's right. One reason why my company kept growing was because Black people kept dying. It was bittersweet—all the work I'd put in had made me the go-to person for this moment. And it was fucked up.

In March 2020, like many who could make the transition, I took my business virtual as the country locked down to slow the spread of COVID-19, a virus that could kill anyone, especially the elderly, but that was wreaking disproportionate havoc on Black and brown communities. Then something else went viral. On May 25, George Floyd, a Black man accused of trying to pass a counterfeit 20-dollar bill at a Minneapolis corner store, was murdered by police officer Derek Chauvin, and it was caught on video.

We'd seen footage like this before—when 12-year-old Tamir Rice was shot within two seconds of law enforcement's arrival while playing with a toy gun; when Eric Garner died in a chokehold after being arrested for selling loose cigarettes; when Philando Castile was shot five times after being pulled over for a minor traffic violation; when fellow Tulsan Terence Crutcher was shot while his hands were visibly in the air; and many, many other times. Whether it was because Floyd's death arrived on the heels of the murders of Ahmaud Arbery, killed while jogging, and Breonna Taylor, killed while sleeping in her bed, or because the whole country was stuck at home hiding from a pandemic with nothing to do but watch their screens, this time people—white people, anyway—responded differently. This time, as the image of an officer pressing his knee against a Black man's neck for eight minutes until the light disappeared from his eyes streamed into our social media feeds, many white Americans finally understood what their fellow Black citizens, as well as many other people of color, have been trying to tell them for, like, forever: that the America many white people live, work, and play in is not the same America in which everyone else exists. The scope of our country's racial inequality finally became visible to people who didn't have to deal with it every day.

When polled in 2020, 76 percent of Americans said that discrimination against racial and ethnic minorities in the U.S. was a "big problem." Seventy-one percent of them were white, 57 percent were conservatives, and 69 percent were whites without college degrees.[3]

In the wake of the global public protests that followed, the country, and my business, changed. Normally, a week or so after a shooting, the calls slow down, but following the death of George Floyd, the phone never stopped ringing. I heard from big tech companies, global corporations, Ivy League universities, and branches of the U.S. military, among others. All asked me to speak to their employees and executives about unconscious bias and to facilitate tough conversations regarding diversity, inclusion, and especially equity. Some were brand new to DEI. Others were suddenly aware their previous efforts weren't enough, sometimes not much more than performative.

I was working 16-hour days, but when I could slow down to read the news, I could see that my new clients weren't the only ones having a massive reckoning. Whereas many companies around the country had long ago stated their dedication to diversity and inclusion, and even taken some steps to prove it, suddenly they were doubling down, making big and sometimes expensive gestures to show their commitment to racial equality. Multiple companies placed full-page ads in newspapers and tweeted messages of solidarity with #BLM and #BlackOutTuesday. Some of these companies went further, aligning their money with values that included combatting systemic racism. Apple committed $100 million to a new Racial Equity and Justice Initiative, part of which would include supporting Black software developers and entrepreneurs; YouTube announced a similar investment in amplifying the work of Black creatives; NASCAR banned the Confederate flag at their events. And this was all happening not because these companies were struck with a massive crisis of conscience, but because their customers were demanding it[4] and calling them out for their lack of diversity and lack of empathy for the inequities and injustices inflicted on BIPOC.

Yet as thrilled as I was that so many companies and organizations seemed ready to have a conversation about race and dismantle racial bias, I knew that many of these efforts were likely doomed to fail. The reality is that though companies frequently do adopt diversity and inclusion initiatives in a sincere effort to make their workforce more representative of the country and to implement equity, many find it harder to accomplish than they'd hoped, and the results disappointing.

Here's why: no matter how well you get the diversity part down by hiring and promoting to achieve a racially, ethnically, religiously, gendered, and sexually-oriented variegated workforce (and most have a long way to go there too), if you don't also build a culture that allows every individual in this diverse group to come to work confident they can be their authentic selves, your company is still operating on an outdated system that crushes innovation and productivity. Worse, when you don't invest the time it takes to build that connected culture, you actually feed a harmful system that saps your company of its spirit and best talent. In fact, you can actually encourage the bias and discrimination you were trying to stamp out. You have to seed Radical Acceptance and learn to be better than your BS wherever you want an inclusive culture to grow, starting with your own backyard.

THE FUTURE OF YOUR BUSINESS DEPENDS ON GETTING DEI RIGHT

It's not just that we're failing as a society if people have to hide who they are in order to professionally succeed. There are practical and financial reasons for helping eradicate the biases, isms, and phobias we bring to work too.

1. At work, people should be using their energy to perform to the best of their abilities. If instead they're expending it trying to make people see, hear, or value them, it doesn't just negatively affect their performance, stamina, and morale, it affects the productivity and experience of their co-workers and team members, which impacts the organization as a whole.

2. The next wave of new employees, members of Gen Z, are the most racially and ethnically diverse generation in U.S. history. They're projected to be majority non-white by 2026,[5] and one in six adult members identify as LGBTQ+.[6] Companies finally took a public stand for diversity and inclusion because their customers demanded it, but in many cases, their employees had been demanding it (often being ignored) for years. That demand is only going to grow. We Gen Xers were taught to be happy to get a job and to keep our personal lives to ourselves, but Millennials and Gen Z expect more from their employers. In 2020, respondents to the Deloitte Global Millennial Survey asserted

that they'd be more inclined to remain loyal to an employer if the business responded to "employee needs," which included diversity and inclusion. Their answers revealed that far from forcing young employees to retreat from their idealism and settle for the jobs they could get in a rough economic climate, the pandemic seemed to harden their opinion that companies should be as much in the business of making society better as they are in making products and services.[7] These workers know that they perform better when they can follow their biorhythms and they want their companies to provide a place to nap onsite. They believe it's inhumane to penalize an employee who needs to tend to a sick family member, so they support child- and dependent-care benefits. They want the company where they work to acknowledge and celebrate Juneteenth, and create a welcoming, supportive environment for all. If you want to attract the best talent, you better get busy creating a company where the best talent is proud and happy to work. Business leaders are no longer being judged merely on what they do really well, but how well they respond and adapt to the issues that really matter.

3. Companies with a more diverse workplace outperform less diverse competitors. McKinsey reports that the most racially and ethnically diverse companies financially outperform industry norms by 35 percent.[8]

4. Companies with a more diverse workplace make more money from innovation. According to Boston Consulting Group (BCG), companies with more diverse management teams have 19 percent higher innovation revenue than those whose diversity is below average.[9]

5. According to a two-year 2015 study of 450 global companies, inclusive companies are "1.7 times more likely to be innovation leaders in their market," and over three years, those that prioritize inclusion show "2.3 times higher cash flow per employee."[10]

6. A 2022 study of work culture by MIT's Sloan School of Management revealed that the leading contributor to toxic work culture included a failure to promote DEI; and toxic work culture was ten times more predictive of high turnover than compensation.[11]

Do you get it now? Successful DEI is the difference between a company that stays stuck in the past and one that's prepared for the future. And the key to successful DEI, the key that's been missing for most companies for so long, even the most well-intentioned ones, is Radical Acceptance.

Radical Acceptance (RA) works simultaneously from all levels, from the inside out, top down, and bottom up. It's what I used to build my award-winning, globally recognized diversity and inclusion speaking, training, and consulting firm, and to become a sought-out community expert on bias—in deep red Oklahoma. It's what gives me the strength to rise above my BS and listen to people's conscious and unconscious biases day in and day out with little judgment and help them free themselves from the invisible shackles holding them back, as well as help everyone they interact with on a personal and professional level. It's what transforms people from being well-meaning but ignorant or frightened bystanders into educated, energized, passionately engaged allies. And it's what my clients around the world have used to live up to their diversity and inclusion pledges and enjoy the positive impacts and competitive advantages that ensue.

I'M NOT A CEO. IS THIS BOOK FOR ME?

I've taught thousands of people at all levels to make their workplaces more supportive, inclusive, and productive, and I can teach you too—even if you're not yet sitting in the C-suite. While other DEI programs focus solely on training execs and middle managers, this one places the responsibility for change on everyone in the company. It's a top-down and bottom-up approach, which is key to circumventing the common bottlenecks that often occur when leaders get intimidated or overwhelmed by DEI issues. Of course, C-level executives in charge of creating policy, HR professionals, and marketers need this book more than anyone. But even if you're not a leader who can make decisions on behalf of the whole company, you can be better than your BS and model RA on your own wherever you work and inspire change. Influencers in all settings—business, community, educational, and faith-based—can have a profound impact at the organizational and the individual level, spreading throughout the company and even beyond.

An organization that builds a BS-free culture where everyone feels safe, secure, valued, and empowered is an organization capitalizing on all its talent and intellectual capital. It's an organization at the top of its competitive game, appealing to the brightest members of the up-and-coming generation that prioritizes diversity and inclusion when choosing where they want to work. And it's an organization boldly setting an example of what it looks like to move beyond the usual Band-Aids and platitudes usually on offer when a social problem is finally too obvious to ignore.

HOW DOES IT WORK?

We achieve Radical Acceptance in two steps, so this book is organized in two parts:

In **Part I, Examine the Roots of Your BS (Radically Accept Yourself)**, you start with a self-awareness deep dive that reveals all your unique gifts as well as your flaws. In particular, you'll learn about your "biasphere"—the circles of influence that shaped your belief systems and biases. They include your family, your peers, your institutions (such as schools, government, and workplaces), and the media. I'll offer questions that prompt you to examine the formative impressions each of these circles of influence had on you. Most people are surprised to discover how frequently the biasphere turns us against ourselves, which is why, for example, so many of us have body image issues, and why many LGBTQ+ people hide their sexual identities. It takes courage to look this closely at yourself and your past, but the insight and awareness you'll gain is akin to waking up untethered outside the Matrix—you become alive in a whole new way.

This isn't a hokey self-help exercise. This is a serious analysis of the forces that determined how you decided you should live, who you should be, and who you expect others to be. The BS fed to you by your biasphere determined your sense of "normal," one of the most restrictive and problematic concepts in human existence. Identify your "normal," and you can identify your "not normal," which means—Bam!—you just unearthed your unconscious biases.

They won't be pretty. They might even be embarrassing. But this is one of the radical things about Radical Acceptance—you're not going to beat yourself up over their existence any more than you might beat yourself up for being left-handed. No judgment allowed. The important thing is that you accept that they exist, because the only problem we can't solve is the one we refuse to see.

Once you've got that, you'll be ready for **Part II, Building a BS-Free Culture (Radically Accept Others)**. Once you identify your biases and see how they influence the way you live and think, you'll be able to more clearly see how they've also influenced the way you respond to and treat others. They explain how "woke" whites could be suspicious of a Black man walking through their neighborhood, and why someone who claims to love all humans might panic if their child comes out. At work, it's why so many leaders hire culture fits instead of culture additions, even though they claim to value diversity, and why team members make unfair assumptions about peers who don't share their background. A lot of us truly believe we accept and respect all people with no regard to race, creed, faith, or gender, but our actions often prove otherwise. Only by dumping our BS can we see it and work harder to live up to our ideals.

To help you get there, in this part of the book you'll learn how to:

- Recognize when your BS manifests as isms and phobias that follow you to work.
- Cure scarcity mentality, a damaging byproduct of fear.
- Validate other people's experiences.
- Become a real ally.
- Engage in micro efforts that can affect change on a macro level.
- Create an environment that fosters a sense of belonging for everybody, that is, "get in where you fit in."
- Abolish group think and create space for diverse ideas.
- Design explicit feedback channels.
- Generate truly inclusive policies that people can trust.
- Spot and stop bullying (it doesn't always look the way you think it does).
- Understand that equality isn't equity; the difference leads to everyone getting what they need.

As you do this work, you'll be prompted to engage in a series of Radical Acts—exercises, questionnaires, diagnostics, and strategies that will allow you to (1) Reassess Your Assets by taking inventory of your organizational culture, including people and policies, (2) Recalibrate Your Alliances by asking you to check whether you're aligning yourself and your values with unfair policies that don't work for everyone, or with the actual humans in the organization, and (3) Radicalize Your Environment. Hear me out. If you're on board with Radical Acceptance, you've acknowledged we need to see sweeping change in how we work together. Radicalizing your environment doesn't require proselytizing or hitting people over the head with your newfound awareness. If you're in a policy-making position, sure, you could make radical rule changes, and I'll suggest some effective ones. But as we've discussed, we can't rely on top-down change alone. The rest of us need to step up too. That means acting as a role model, calling out problematic scenarios or language when they come across your radar, standing firm when you get pushback, and applying everything you'll learn in this book to the real world. It's about taking responsibility to fix or at least shine a light on what's not working in your traditional work culture whenever possible. That kind of courage is contagious. A whole team of people with that kind of courage? That's a radicalized environment.

Throughout this book, I'll share stories of companies that have called me in for help. There was the CEO shocked to discover that her young, progressive team wasn't quite so progressive when it came to sharing status and resources; the nonprofit dedicated to protecting at-risk youth with staff members who didn't feel safe coming out at work; the oil company whose lone female pipefitter spent years gritting her teeth as her male supervisor double-checked her work and no one else's; the manager so afraid of saying the wrong thing, he'd decided to avoid speaking to his Black employees altogether; the transportation company that kept finding nooses hanging in their maintenance center; and many others. Resolving these conflicts and unearthing the BS that caused them wasn't always an easy or smooth process, but each time, introducing Radical Acceptance helped break stagnation and set these organizations up for more harmonious, productive, prosperous paths.

Radical Acceptance enables people to enter into conversations that feel dangerous, yet are necessary for growth and progress. It keeps us from judging people for their questions, their confusion, or their mistakes—even as we refuse to let them off the hook. It proves that empathy is a strength, not a weakness. It's the bridge, the "&" between diversity & inclusion, that allows you to connect and build the kind of open, honest, and productive culture that makes yours the type of organization everyone wants to work for, and you the kind of colleague everyone wants to work with.

LET'S DO THIS!

Corporate America is engaged in a period of massive change, so while we're remaking the work environment, let's really remake the work environment. Because the system isn't broken. The system is working exactly as it was designed. Which means the only solution is to tear it completely down.

The systemic racism in the U.S. used to make me believe this country wasn't built for people like me. Today, a national reckoning and the business world's commitment to diversity, equity, and inclusion has some people scared shitless the future won't be made for them. They don't have to be. Radical Acceptance replaces fear with confidence, and the threat of scarcity with a sense of security. Through this process, thousands of leaders, managers, and employees have successfully started breaking down the biases and racism that exists in their workplaces, and reveling in the improved morale, retention, productivity, and profits that result. Best of all, whereas once they used to unwittingly carry their biases into the workplace, now they're consciously carrying the lessons they've learned at work out into the world and applying them toward their daily interactions with friends, family, and faith communities. Business may be the engine of our country, but people are the heart of business. When the corporate world becomes better than its BS and empowers everyone to show up to work as their best, most authentic selves, the benefits will cascade outward. That's when America will finally fulfill its spectacular promise.

PART I

EXAMINE THE ROOTS OF YOUR BS

(RADICALLY ACCEPT YOURSELF)

CHAPTER 1

WE'RE ALL FULL OF BS

A guy walks into a bar and sits next to a woman who is tired AF after a nonstop series of training sessions at a big bank in downtown Chicago. Her exhaustion must show, because he asks, "Long day?"

"Yep," she replies, and she's got another one planned for tomorrow.

"I'm here for work too," he says. He introduces himself as Mike.

The woman, always networking and looking for her next gig, asks, "What kind of work do you do?"

Mike explains that he manages a high-end custom construction company. He spends a lot of time on the road, traveling throughout the U.S. making sure the job is well done. She tells him she's a trainer.

"What kind of training?" he asks.

She offers her usual playful response. "I teach adults how to respect each other."

He laughs. "What?"

"It's true," she says, smiling. "I get paid the big bucks to remind adults to treat each other with common courtesy and respect."

"Bullshit!" he says, his eyes wide.

Now she's the one laughing. "You just summed it up. I literally teach people to get rid of their BS."

They continue to laugh and make small talk at the bar, then decide to toast to one very long day. He orders another beer; she raises her glass of white wine. After clinking glasses, he looks at the woman and says with admiration, "Wow. You are such a credit to your race."

The woman—who is Black—puts her drink down hard, and sharply turns her face to him. "What did you say, white boy?"

The man pauses, then quickly smiles and says in what he seems to think is a reassuring tone, "No, let me explain. See, most Black people don't want to work really hard; they just want things handed to them. Not you, though!"

The Black woman fixes him with a stony look. "You know this isn't going well, right?"

The Black woman was me, and no, this isn't a bar joke. It was 2018, but this encounter with a young professional in his thirties was a reminder that there are a lot of folks out there still stuck in 1962. Not that I needed another reminder. As a diversity, equity, and inclusion (DEI) expert and consultant, it's my job to not only confront this reality but help others see it too. My work as a culture connector—during which I encourage employees to honestly (often anonymously) share their perspectives and opinions about topics such as race, gender, age, and sexual orientation—reveals that the majority of people, most of whom would vigorously deny they were prejudiced or discriminatory, have thoughts like these racing through their cranium:

- Black parents who give their kids weird names aren't doing them any favors.

- Why do those men keep their beards? They look like terrorists.

- You can't get promoted in accounting unless you're Jewish.

- What's with these women having babies and expecting us to cover for them while they take time off?

- I wish the company would quit hiring people with Spanish accents. They're too hard to understand.

- Another one wearing a cross. You know they're all homophobes.

- Some people seem to think they can just flaunt their gayness at the office. It's not appropriate.

- I can't believe this guy wants me to use female pronouns when speaking to him. How the hell am I supposed to remember that, when he looks like a man?

- Millennials are lazy.

- Old people need to make room for the rest of us. Why don't they just retire already?

Still, my new drinking buddy's racist statement threw me for a loop. We'd been having an awesome time together, and now the night was ruined. The weight of 400 years of history, plus one long-ass workday, settled around my neck and shoulders, and all I wanted to do was curse him out and go back to my hotel room so I could be alone.

But I didn't curse him out, because in that moment, I had a choice: I could be right, or I could win.

Telling Mike off would have felt satisfying and right. But after I'd stormed out of the bar, what would have happened? He'd have probably sat there feeling defensive. Maybe he would have decided that I was the one who'd created a problem where there was none by being over-sensitive, or blowing his words out of proportion, or mis-understanding what he meant. Because he knew he wasn't racist, he'd tell himself. He wasn't a bad person.

Yet as much as I wasn't in the mood to work overtime, wasn't this exactly what I'd signed up for 25 years ago when I'd committed to teaching people about inequal-ity, diversity, and inclusion? What if I could open Mike's eyes and help him see his racist BS? What if by walking away, I was missing a chance to help him understand why his words had cut so deeply? What if I, a Black, bisexual, ex-preacher's wife, could move the needle just a little bit and spare anyone else in his path the disrespect he'd just unloaded on me? That would be a win. And I was willing to sacrifice being right for the win.

So I stayed. He didn't understand what he'd done wrong, but Mike did know he'd hurt me, and for that he apologized. I accepted and suggested that a great way to make it up to me would be to let me explain why what he'd said was problematic. He agreed. In fact, he offered to buy me dinner. Over the course of our meal, I pointed out that Black people have always worked hard. I mean, let's think about how and why we were brought to this country in the first place. And I gave him a rapid-fire history lesson—encompassing Jim Crow laws, lynching, redlining, separate but equal, the Red Summer and the destruction of Black Wall Street, the "war on drugs" that was actually a war on poor people and Black folks, voter suppression, and the structurally racist systems that hinder the political, professional, and economic success of BIPOC to such an extent that whites hold 85 percent of all upper-level executive jobs[1] and Blacks receive less than 1 percent of venture capital[2]—to demonstrate that we have never had anything handed to us. Finally, I explained that the praise he thought he'd given me was actually a backhanded compliment (or a microaggression), because what he was really saying was that most Black people were not worthy of respect, but somehow, I was different. Except if he spoke with and interacted with more Black people, he'd know that people like me were legion; we just face obstacles that never even cross his radar.

I listened too. That's how I learned how Mike, a decent and cool guy, could say something so blatantly racist to me without giving it a second thought. He had grown up in a small, predominantly white town and hadn't spent a lot of time around Black people for most of his life. He'd been taught his racist ideas from a young age, and it had never occurred to him to question them. When he wasn't traveling, he lived in a house at the end of a mile-long driveway, so far from the neighbors, he said, he could sit on the porch naked if he wanted to. I told him that the problem wasn't who he was or where he came from, but that the racism and prejudice he'd absorbed and spit back out was built into the very foundations of our society, causing pain and obstacles to me and millions of other

BIPOC every day. And then I told him how he could be a part of the solution.

Mike's reaction to our conversation alternated between surprise, shock, embarrassment, and frustration. In total we spent four to five hours together that night. I got a big steak dinner and a bottle of wine out of that conversation, but more important, I made an ally.

Three years later, I still occasionally get texts from Mike, who likes to tell me about moments when he's spoken up when witnessing racism or bigotry. What's exciting to me is that these stories aren't just taking place in his hometown or with family members, where you might expect. He's bravely speaking up at work, calling out racist or bigoted jokes, remarks, and incidents that could cause people to feel uncomfortable or invisible on job sites. He's made a concerted effort to create a better work environment for his team, one where everyone feels safe and is treated with respect and consideration. Within minutes, anyone who works with him knows racism, prejudice, and bigotry won't be tolerated. And in the time he's been actively confronting racism, bigotry, and prejudice, without passing judgment and from a place of compassion and understanding—after all, not long ago he was saying some of the same crap he now shuts down—he has not lost a single employee, client, or colleague.

What did I use to help this guy, as oblivious to his entrenched racism as anyone I've ever met, recognize that his beliefs about Black people and pretty much anyone who wasn't just like him were false and harmful, and inspire him to engage in anti-racist work . . . at work?

The same thing I teach my clients every day: how to use Radical Acceptance to become better than their BS.

YOU'VE GOT QUESTIONS, I'VE GOT ANSWERS

What's Radical Acceptance? It's the practice of welcoming and embracing our full humanity, without BS, full stop.

What's so radical about it? It's transformative. Being better than our BS requires unlearning much of what we've been taught by the people we love and the institutions we trust most. The result is a dramatic shift in perspective that makes the world look completely different from the one we thought we lived in.

What's BS? Oh, it's bullshit, for sure. More specifically, though, it's the often invisible, always powerful belief systems we've been steeped in since birth. These belief systems established the rules and standards against which we judge ourselves and others, leading us to unconsciously show preference for people who fit within those rules and standards, and develop biases against those who don't. We express those biases as racism, sexism, ageism, homophobia, and other prejudices. Silently, insidiously, our BS shapes how we feel about ourselves, how we perceive the world, and consequently, how we interact with others. And with 6 out of 10 employed Americans saying they regularly witness bias or discrimination at work,[3] our interactions on the job (and in bars) clearly leave room for improvement.

Now, many American businesses are finally—finally—prioritizing and investing in making their workplaces more diverse, equitable, and inclusive. That's a great thing. Unfortunately, they're being sabotaged by the same kind of BS that kept Mike from being able to see his racism for what it was, resulting in conflict, tension, and high turnover that keeps diversity rates stagnant and employees feeling isolated and unsupported. BS is the number one reason why so many well-intentioned DEI initiatives fail. It underpins a problem inherent in most American businesses, even those that sincerely want to improve their rates of diversity and inclusion, even those like yours: you're working within a white, hetero framework that is so deeply embedded into your culture and society, you don't even realize it's there.

WHAT GETS IN THE WAY

The obstacle most American businesses face when trying to implement a culture of inclusion is, well, the entire foundation of American business. DEI initiatives can't work until people stop clinging to the beliefs and old standards that prop up the status quo. Our codes for "professional" and "normal" were born out of a white construct, created by and for straight, white men. That's why even in spaces where colleagues and supervisors are certain they've cultivated a welcoming environment, many BIPOC and LGBTQ+ employees struggle to feel accepted. Because to belong in the majority of workplaces, you still have to come from the right background. You have to speak a certain way. You have to dress in a certain style and wear your hair "appropriately." It's assumed you're attracted to people of the opposite sex or that you are a Christian. In sum, if you want to professionally succeed, you have to fit a mold. That mold usually frequently looks and sounds like straight, white, thin, able-bodied, church-going America.

Are most straight, white, thin, able-bodied church-going people going around actively trying to alienate or hurt their BIPOC or LGBTQ+ co-workers? No. Yet they unintentionally do it all the time. Well-intentioned people know how to recognize and call out overt racism or bigotry (even if they don't always have the courage to do so). But many can't even recognize the casual, nuanced biases, isms, and phobias they or their peers bring to work every day that create toxic environments and communities. They can't see it because they've been steeped in the BS of racism and bigotry from the day they were born—not because the people who raised them meant to, but because the entire system we live in is built on it. They're like the fish in David Foster Wallace's famous commencement speech, who after being asked by another fish, "How's the water?" turn to each other and ask, "What's water?" This blindness and lack of understanding is why:

- Almost half of all LGBTQ+ employees believe that being fully out at work could hurt their career prospects (and less than 0.3 percent of Fortune 500 directors are openly LGBTQ+).[4]

- According to a 2019 GlassDoor survey, more than half of LGBTQ+ employees say they have experienced or witnessed anti-LGBTQ+ comments by co-workers.[5]

- Black women are 80 percent more likely than non-Black women to agree with the statement, "I have to change my hair from its natural state to fit in at the office."[6]

- Despite the huge number of workplaces that went remote in 2020, the number of workplace discrimination claims only dropped 7 percent.[7]

- In a worldwide customer workforce survey, only 6 out of 10 believed people with "different backgrounds" could succeed at the companies where they worked.[8]

For people employed at companies where they don't believe they'll be accepted for who they are, or who fear repercussions to their career if they reveal their true selves, going to work every day can feel like putting on a costume. Not just a little face paint, but a full head-to-toe costume, like the one worn by Anthony Daniels, whom you know as C-3PO. His 60-lb rubber-and-metal gold suit[9] was bolted on to him, and so heavy and stiff that for the few months of shooting *Star Wars*, he couldn't sit down between film takes. Because he was completely covered up, "people eventually forgot he was a real person, treating him like a prop."[10] Daniels got so frustrated that people couldn't see him, he handed out custom-made matchboxes to the crew inscribed with the words, "3PO IS HUMAN!"

Imagine feeling like that every single day of your working life.

I guarantee that people you know and like—peers, supervisors, assistants, employees—do. And their pain has possibly been exacerbated if your company has gone fully remote or allows remote options. Many who didn't already feel free to be themselves at work are now wearing their costume for hours at home too. Speaking out against the problem, even in a time of supposed corporate woke-ness, didn't make things better. On the contrary, retaliation charges—accusations of firing, harassing, demoting, or otherwise punishing employees for filing complaints or opposing discrimination in other ways[11]—accounted for over half the discrimination charges filed in 2020.[12]

We cannot continue to miss out on the gifts and talents of millions of our colleagues because we can't figure out how to make them feel safe and empowered.

YOUR NEW SKILL SET

Unconscious bias is a pervasive, corrosive, systemic problem that exists in virtually every workplace, undermining the business and everyone who works there in ways its leaders can't see. And for years we've been told it's an impossible problem to solve. After all, how do you shore up a weakness when you're not even aware you have it? Well, you start by believing the people who tell you it's there and that their lives are harder because of it. And then you commit to learning something new, even if you didn't know you needed to.

I hosted a roundtable event for a company in which their supervisors were asked to watch four online informational videos and then given the chance to AMA—ask me anything. Literally, any questions they had about racism, BIPOC, working in a diverse environment, I was there to talk about it. Our system allowed participants to remain anonymous. And yet, even with promised anonymity, I couldn't get anyone to talk. "C'mon people. I know this is uncomfortable, but this is how we make progress. I know some of you may be uninterested or indifferent. I know some you are worried and may be even harboring some fear, but I need you to talk." Finally, after several silent, uncomfortable moments, a participant did speak up. Identifying herself as a Black woman, she was irritated. "You know, I have a problem with this. They're so scared and you're bending over backward trying to make them feel better. You know what? I'm scared all the time, no one does anything to make me feel better, and I still show up. I do what needs to be done. Shouldn't they?" I understood. Black people and other POC have been showing up despite their fear their entire lives. Every day, we enter rooms full of people who don't look or sound like us, wondering if we're going to be accepted, or if we'll have to work extra hard to lessen people's suspicions and earn their respect. Will today be easy, or will we get hit with an insult or slight that stings, however unintentionally? White people may worry about whether a presentation will go well, or be justifiably nervous about entering a room full of strangers, but these are isolated incidents in a life overall constructed in such a way that wherever they go, no one will question if they belong. For professionals of color, that's not a given, and it gets even harder for those aspiring to the higher levels of white-collar America. POC develop a skill set at a young age to help them cope with those scenarios. In general, white people just don't have to.

That's not to say POC don't have their own biases and bigotries, even against individuals who share their race or ethnic group but deviate from a culturally or socially con-structed "ideal" or "norm." That's why Radical Acceptance is a skill set everyone needs to learn. I'm happy to be your first teacher if you'll let me.

WHY RADICAL ACCEPTANCE WORKS

The Radical Acceptance method is salt to the slug of bias and succeeds when others don't because it's two-pronged. On an individual level, it gives us the tools to see our BS and replace it with mindfulness, patience, kind-ness, forgiveness, and deep listening and communication skills, all necessary for achieving understanding. No one can legislate unconscious bias out of people's hearts and minds, but when we're willing to do the inner, personal work of unlearning what we were taught since childhood,

Radical Acceptance grants us the self-awareness to identify the BS that causes it.

But awareness is not enough. Once we know what BS feeds our fears and fuels our sense of threat, we're ready for the next step, what I call the outer work—changing how we interact with others. Radical Acceptance allows us to listen better, make space for people to be themselves, and give them room to shine and excel. It also gives us the courage to step up and speak out when we see people or policies not doing the same, and the vision to offer solutions, all while—and this is key!—leading with love, trust, respect, and inclusivity.

When we—executives, managers, and employees—bring that person to work, we change the culture around us. When we bring that person to work at a company committed to anti-racism and promoting and valuing diversity, that's where we see a truly inclusive culture develop.

Once you rise above your own BS and radically accept yourself with all your imperfections, you can extend that Radical Acceptance to everyone else who works with you, thus putting a stop to your organization's BS—the unfair expectations, double standards, and biases built into its foundation. As the culture of Radical Acceptance extends from person to person, it makes employees feel safe. They can breathe. People who can breathe perform better. They voice their ideas and share their experience and perspectives. They cross pollinate, which allows companies to produce better goods and services. Radical Acceptance allows leaders to create a culture that welcomes and accepts everyone as they are, freeing their creative spirit, their enthusiasm, and their dedication to the job and the company's mission.

Now, of course no one employee can single-handedly stamp out racism, bigotry, homophobia, or prejudice in an environment where those elements are perpetually and intentionally reinforced from the top. But no company can change unless its people do too. Each level of the organization has to work together. Radical Acceptance is the catalyst that transforms company culture from the inside out. Ultimately, that's how we change the world, for social transformations are simply personal transformations at scale. One Mike, one Risha, one you at a time, Radical Acceptance can jump-start the change we really do want to see.

A WORD TO THE WOKE

Maybe you're thinking, you know, I grew up in a diverse city, I have friends from all over, and I would never say something racist. See the BLM sign in my yard? I don't need this book.

Make no mistake, it's not only blatant racists and bigots undermining companies' diversity and inclusion goals. There are plenty of woke people unknowingly being led around by their BS too.

See, most Mikes don't know they're Mikes. And even if we have nothing in common with Mike, even when we've made a thoughtful effort not to contribute to the problem of racism and discrimination, even when we've read the right educational books and watched the right illuminating documentaries, we can't counteract our BS until we've had the courage to examine it. You heard that right. It takes a brave person to turn over the rock of their beliefs to see what unconscious biases lie beneath, because we might not like what we find. But as always, you can't fix a problem if you don't know it's there.

What was impressive about Mike wasn't just that he was willing to change the way he ran his job sites and interacted with his colleagues and peers, but also that he was even willing to consider that there was anything he needed to change in the first place. Believe me, there are a lot of so-called tolerant people that get their backs up when someone suggests they have more work to do if they want to be a part of the solution and not the problem. You know how I know? There was a time when I was suspicious of all white people. There was a time when I thought homosexuality was a sin. It wasn't until 2015 that I finally acknowledged that I was unconsciously biased toward the trans community. One time, my religious bias prompted me to assume a dinner guest was a Satan worshiper. Oh yes, I've hauled around my fair share of BS. That's how I know the lessons in this book work—I've been my own student.

THE REWARD

Not long ago, I made myself available by Zoom to a group of managers who'd watched a number of my online training videos on the topic of BS as part of a mandatory DEI training, to make sure they had a chance to ask me questions about what they'd seen or how to proceed next. Most of the participants in these forums use my online tool that allows them to air their thoughts while remaining anonymous. But in this meeting, there was one person who was willing to reveal himself. He told me, "I've read a lot about racism in the workplace and unconscious bias over the years and tried hard to walk the walk, so I didn't think anything you could say would apply to me. Your videos made me think about where I started and why the work was so hard for me at first. I've been feeling good about where I've gotten, but those videos helped me see how much more there is for me to do." Later, this same manager sent me an e-mail thanking me again, saying that what he'd learned in our training had helped him better connect with his team. "I've had so many tough but great conversations."

Tough but great. Like anything else worthwhile, from body-changing exercise to intense skill-building practice, that's what successful DEI efforts and implementations feel like. We have to be willing to work through the discomfort in order to reap our rewards.

Wait, what?

That's right, it isn't just POC, transgender people, religious minorities, or whoever isn't just like you who benefit when you embrace Radical Acceptance. It won't only help you make your workplace better for others, it will make it better for you. Radical Acceptance is the surest, most lasting way to break down the BS that causes the miscommunication, friction, and tension that causes people to feel ostracized or judged. The more people are willing to acknowledge and address the biases inherent in their belief systems, the more those biases will dissipate, and the better our work environments will become. People who believe their contributions will be acknowledged and appreciated, who feel valued for their efforts, and who believe they are respected and will have the same opportunities to advance as anyone else, perform better and earn businesses more money. They have more energy and stamina to do their jobs. They stick around longer. They feel more loyalty to their employer. They work better with their peers, which makes the whole team more productive and more fun to work with. On top of that, Radical Acceptance not only makes our workplaces better, but it also makes our work culture at large better. Our country, better. Our future, better. Dismantling systemic racism isn't about diminishing any one person or group's ability to succeed. It's simply about accepting— and empowering—everyone.

GETTING STARTED

Mike didn't mean to hurt me. He genuinely thought he was patting me on the back even as he slapped me in the face. Yet while he may seem like an extreme example of casual, ignorant racism, I assure you we all have a little Mike in us.

Don't believe me? Let's find out. Answer these five questions:

1. Have you ever made assumptions about people based upon their race/ethnicity, gender, sexual orientation, religion, age, socioeconomic status, or another characteristic?

2. Have you ever qualified a person's value based on those characteristics? For example, have you ever thought, She's pretty for someone that big? Or been surprised at someone's excellent manners . . . considering they're so country?

3. Have you ever felt uncomfortable or experienced a negative feeling or reaction

around certain groups or individuals based upon any of those characteristics?

4. When hearing or reading a story or article, do you assume the characters or subjects are white, straight, and identify as male or female unless it's stated otherwise?

5. Do you think everyone has the same opportunities for success and fulfillment?

Answering yes to any of these reveals that yep, you're full of BS.

Spoiler alert: everyone who's honest says yes to at least one, usually more (including me). And that's okay! To have BS is to be human. But to have gas is to be human too, and yet no one willingly goes around stinking up their co-workers' air space when they know there's something they can do about it. The inevitability of unconscious BS doesn't let us off the hook from trying to get rid of it. Sure, we all fall on a spectrum, and some people have more BS than others, but if you haven't thoroughly, unsparingly examined yours and committed to neutralizing, you're probably not as different from pre-RA Mike as you think. Most of us have much more BS than we realize, even when we strive to do the right thing. We're all insulated from each other in some ways, even those who grow up in big, richly diverse cities. We grow up in different cultures and faiths. We have blind spots. We can't know each other's minds. We're quick to judge.

But we can try harder to be better.

RISE TO MEET YOUR OWN BAR

Our answers to the questions above often reveal that we have reactions and behaviors that are so natural, so automatic, we don't even recognize them in the moment. But if we can't recognize them, how can we say with any certainty that these behaviors and reactions aren't infiltrating our interactions and perpetuating harm in small or even in big ways? We can't. In my experience, most people don't go through life wishing to cause anyone else pain. Taking this moment to examine your biases and analyze their origins is your chance to make sure you're living up to your own dearest, self-professed values.

The techniques you're about to learn won't teach you how to change other people, but they will show you how to inspire change. They'll teach you to change the way you speak and listen. They'll change how you interpret what you see. They'll reveal that when you respond with openness and curiosity toward others, they will often respond in kind. When you extend general good vibes and model nonjudgment, you can lower suspicion and inspire others to be less judgmental too. This is how we make diversity our strength and turn a skeptical, combative, disconnected culture into a trusting, supportive, inclusive one. I've seen this transformation happen. In fact, I've gone through it myself, using these same techniques to tackle my own biased, transphobic, and judgmental BS.

It can be scary to leave your BS behind; not everyone will approve or understand. Challenging your or anyone else's BS can require deep wells of courage, strength of character, and persistence. The process can often separate us from our usual tribe. I've had to tread that line carefully in my own family and had to pick and choose my battles. No matter how committed we are to improving our own interactions with and beliefs about others, it's up to each individual to decide how far they're willing to go to help their friends and loved ones see when they have some room for improvement as well. In some cases, the best we can do is be the best role model possible. Believe me, you may not think people are watching, but they are. Ask anyone who has walked this path, and they'll tell you the risk, and the reward, was worth it.

CHAPTER 2

ASSESS YOUR BS

In 1994, I was a college student at Kansas State. Going to school there wasn't much different from going to school in my mostly white hometown of Sapulpa, Oklahoma. Many Black people who grow up in predominantly white spaces develop an extra friendly persona to help counteract any negative biases associated with their skin color that form before they can even open their mouths. Lucky for me, my natural personality is the type that doesn't meet too many strangers, and I was an athlete and heavily involved in sports, which gave me an in, so I usually got along fine with everyone. Then came the day when I was sitting in the student union and the O. J. Simpson verdict was announced. Not guilty. The reaction in the room was electric. Black folks were happy, cheering, and pumping their fists in the air. White folks were pissed and horrified at the Black students' reactions. How could they be happy that a likely murderer had gotten off scot-free?

Black students understood this was probably an unjust ruling given all the evidence against the former football star, but they couldn't help seeing O. J.'s freedom as payback for every innocent Black man who'd been locked away or executed before him. There was a long history of Black and brown men condemned to unduly harsh sentences for minor crimes while white defendants often walked free or received shorter sentences for the same thing. Where was their white friends' outrage then? So many people jailed for nothing, and they're mad about one man getting off? How could white people not get that when an unjust system means the innocent who look like you usually lose, even an abhorrent prize still feels like a win?

Nothing got out of hand, but it was tense in that room. I understood why the white students reacted the way they did. They weren't necessarily wrong. But I also took note of the students who couldn't or wouldn't understand where their Black peers were coming from, and it left me with a bad feeling. Be careful, I reminded myself, for long before I'd learned that white people, even the nice ones, weren't to be trusted.

Four years later, after I'd graduated, University of Wyoming student Matthew Shepard was found tied to a barbed wire fence, tortured, and left for dead in the near-freezing cold. He died of his injuries six days later. He was 21 years old, and he was gay. His assailants, Aaron McKinney and Russell Henderson, had lured Shepard into their truck with the intent to rob him by pretending to be gay. A detective testified that McKinney's girlfriend told him that McKinney had admitted he'd brutally attacked Shepard because he'd put his hand on McKinney's leg and, "Well, you know how I feel about gays."[1] By this time, I was starting to work through my sexuality, though still not able or willing to put a label on it. It was hard enough being Black. Black and bisexual? No thank you. I already knew enough about the vicious bigotry and prejudice that existed against homosexuals to know that coming out could be dangerous, but the circumstances surrounding Shepard's tragic death scared the hell out of me. So that's how some folks treated people like me? Got it.

How about you? Depending on your age, there are any number of events that could have shaped your interpretation of the world and the people in it based solely on how your family and social circle reacted to them. When Susan Smith accused a (fictional) Black man of hijacking her car and drowning her two children. When men from the Middle East flew planes into the twin towers. When teenager Trayvon Martin was killed, or during the course of George Zimmerman's trial. What reactions did you hear or see online from people you cared about with regard to the uptick in violence against Asians and Asian Americans when they became scapegoats for the spread of COVID-19, referred to in some circles as the "Kung Flu"?

The impact is felt deepest when we're children and the only lens we have to look through is the one handed to us by our families. When my nephew was about seven years old, we were driving on the highway together when a woman's car started swerving erratically. I thought she might have fallen asleep or was texting, and was debating calling the police, until I saw there was already a cop driving along her other side. Out loud, I wondered, "Why isn't he pulling her over?" My nephew replied, so quick, "Because she's white." Now I was the one to almost drive off the road. I asked him why he'd said that, but he didn't want to tell me for fear of getting in trouble. I had to promise him I wouldn't get angry. Finally, he said, "Because cops don't like Black people. They like white people."

This was right around the time when unarmed Terence Crutcher, a Black man, was shot by a white police officer in Tulsa while his hands were raised in the air. I knew siblings from the Crutcher family, and his death shook everyone in town. My family and I talked through our communal grief a lot in those days when we'd get together, venting our anger about a system that seemed to train cops to be hair-trigger ready to obliterate Black lives, while they managed to bring violent white people—many armed or guilty of disobeying police orders—into custody whole and unharmed. Less than a year later, 24-year-old Jerry Lee Newman, a white man, stole a utility truck from my hometown, led police on a highway chase, crashed through the Tulsa airport gate onto the runway, then slammed through a fence onto another highway where he continued going the wrong way, plowed head-on into a car, killing the driver, before fleeing the scene on foot. Somehow, despite the fact that Newman had aimed the stolen car at the cops trying to stop him, officers were able to make an arrest without hurting him.[2]

We saw the seven-year-old playing video games in the living room as we talked about these cases, but we never thought he was actually listening. Unfortunately, he was, and what I learned from our conversation in the car was that the message my nephew absorbed was that cops were out to kill people who looked like him. That was dangerous. It was a mindset that could affect the way he thought of and responded to police officers for the rest of his life. I knew right then that I had to backpedal and give him context, walking a fine line between explaining that of course all cops don't hate Black people, but that as a cute Black boy who would grow up to be a strong Black man in a country that frequently portrays such men as violent, thuggish, and to be feared, he was going to have to move through the world carefully.

White people can't be trusted. Straight people condone violence against the LGBTQ+ community. As you can see, in my younger days I was carrying around a lot of BS—harmful beliefs and biases. But even though objectively these beliefs aren't true, at the time they felt real. It's also BS that cops hate all Black people, but my nephew couldn't know that, especially at such a young age. And remember Mike? Like many people who say racist, sexist, or bigoted things, Mike had no idea that what he'd said to me reflected his BS. But remember—the wokest of the woke are loaded with BS too. White people. People of color. LGBTQ+ people. We just can't see it. Mike, and you, and I, and my nephew, and everyone on this planet, are products of the socializing agents that formed us and our beliefs. Together, those forces form what I call our "biasphere."

WHAT'S A BIASPHERE?

A biasphere is the culmination of the circles of influences we're steeped in at any given time that shape our perspective of the world and form our biases. Our biasphere is particularly powerful when we're young, but even when we leave one, we enter another. Sometimes we can't see our BS because we don't want to. But frequently, even when we try, our biasphere gets in the way. Not only are we products of our biasphere, it also actively blinds us to the biases it inspires.

Unless you know where and how to look.

THE FIVE RINGS

There are five socializing agents that form the rings of our biasphere: family, peers and friends, schools or government, religion, and mass media. These institutions can have huge positive influences on us, but even at their best, they can also simultaneously load us up with tons of negative shit and harmful thinking about certain groups of people, often without us realizing it, often even when we know and love individuals from those groups.

For example, when I was growing up, one of my best friends was white. You could find her family in our backyard at every barbecue, and we girls spent so much time at each other's homes, I thought of her father as a second dad. It never occurred to me that he gave my skin color or anyone else's a second thought until we got to high school, when my friend showed interest in dating my cousin. Her father hit the roof (though he never articulated why), and a rift opened between us. He never knew because I never said anything, but I was hurt. I mean, I was Black, and he'd never had a problem with me. He was friends with my father. My cousin was cut from the same cloth as us. Why wouldn't this man even give him a chance? My friend couldn't offer any insight because he wouldn't explain himself to her, either. As an adult I tried to ask him about his reaction years earlier to that interracial relationship. He couldn't offer a straight answer, but I already knew. At some point, no matter how comfortable he'd become with interracial friendships, he'd learned that romantic relationships between white women and Black men should be treated with skepticism.

Later, in my early twenties, I became close friends with a white woman who played in my nearly all-Black basketball league. When a new league formed, I was invited to play but she wasn't, and she wound up playing on a mostly white team. One day we played against each other, and my team beat hers. By a lot. Riding home from the game together, we got in a fight that ended with her yelling, "You were acting like one of them!"

"What do you mean by that?" I asked.

"You know what I mean." I could tell by the startled look on her face when I forced her to explain herself that she realized how awful her words sounded, but the damage was done. I thought my heart would break.

Neither of these people would have ever described themselves as racist. I wouldn't have, either, if I hadn't witnessed their BS myself. Both sincerely cared about me, I'm sure of it. But that's because they'd met me under circumstances where I didn't seem threatening and they'd been able to get to know me, even as they carried biases that prevented them from extending that acceptance and trust to groups of people like me. In their minds, I was different from the rest of "them." It hurt. And yet by that time I, too, was already moving through the world with the bias about white people I mentioned above, as well as others.

There's little reason to believe that the bias that makes someone uncomfortable when their daughter dates a Black man won't affect their thinking when deciding whether a Black employee is good enough for a promotion, or for someone who won't date short men to subconsciously eliminate an excellent job candidate when they meet for an in-person interview and he's only 5'4". No one leaves their shit at the office door (or the Zoom waiting room), so it's crucial that we examine ours closely. That's the only way we're able to dig up our biases and start tearing them down. To do that, we have to know how and where our formative biaspheres were created. There are questions you can ask yourself to help you pinpoint how your circles of influence taught you to see the world and judge others. Mind you, the goal here isn't to fix something that's wrong with you. It's an exercise in self-awareness to get a clear picture of who we are, and why.

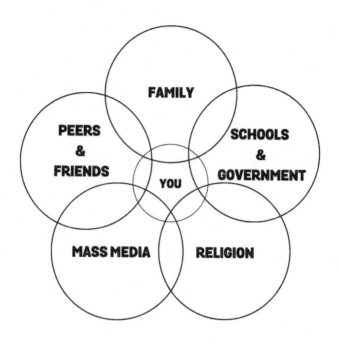

Ring #1: Family

Our immediate families are our primary teachers about how to navigate the world. And I think it's important to remember that most of the time, whether today we agree with their tactics or not, these individuals were simply trying to protect us. I know that was the case with my grandmother Ola Mae. Grandma was known everywhere as the kindest person in the world. She and Jesus were best friends. Seriously, she was a gansta for God and she would never have consciously, willfully taught me anything she thought denigrated others. Yet as a child, Grandma made it clear that there was a mysterious, negative presence in town that I needed to do my darndest to avoid and appease. When I was learning to read, write, and count, she kept me indoors many days in the summer to tutor me because she was worried that "they" wouldn't teach me the way they taught everyone else. One day I heard her speaking on the phone, but she didn't sound like herself. She sounded . . . formal. When I asked her why she was talking so weird, she quickly brushed the question aside and stated, "That's just how you have to talk to them." Them again, huh? Who were these "theys" and "thems"? I got the answer in a Walmart parking lot. We got out of the car, when she suddenly grabbed me and started jamming her hands into my waistband to tuck my shirt into my shorts. I resisted like crazy because I was looking cute and this wasn't that kind of short set, but she was having none of it. "Hush! They'll think you ain't being raised right." She got me presentable (in her mind), then headed briskly toward the store. I scurried next to her, begging, "Who, Grandma? Who is 'they'?" She slowed down just enough to give me an exasperated look: "White folks, chile," before moving on.

White people? Oh my God, white people? Our town was 90 percent white! They were everywhere! And they didn't like me? What was I going to do?

I had never had a negative experience with a white person before, but one of the people I loved most in the world said I needed to be afraid, that they were going to hurt me. Of course I listened.

I don't remember my grandma ever saying a derogatory word about anyone when I was young, white or otherwise. But she had to teach her granddaughter how to navigate this world, and she believed that I was going to have to know more, dress nicer, speak more elegantly, and be all-around better than any white person around me if I was going to succeed in white society. That was how a lot of us with Black grandparents born in the 1920s were taught. If I'm really being honest, Black kids today are still being taught that.

My parents had the same instinct to protect their daughter from white people. In elementary school I was invited to a birthday party, but worried there would be no other Black children present and unsure of how I'd be treated, they wouldn't let me go. The day after the party, the birthday girl and her mom drove into my Black neighborhood to give me a piece of cake and a balloon. Mom and Dad didn't forbid me from associating with white people—for example, they voiced no objection to my eighth-grade boyfriend, who was white—but they proceeded with caution and urged me to do the same.

Meanwhile, though my parents were hyper aware of any racism and bigotry toward their daughter, they sometimes struggled with their own. When my dad and his friends got together, I'd hear them refer to white people as "peckerwoods." At the time I didn't know what it meant, but obviously it wasn't a compliment. I chalked it up to one more reason to be cautious around white people. I figured out early that as far as my dad was concerned, the only group more suspect than white people were gay people. My mother was close friends with a gay guy, and my father was so rude, referring to him as a "fag" to his face, she started arranging to see her friend somewhere other than our house. When I was in middle school, a man started walking around the neighborhood in women's clothes. It was the '80s, and there he'd be in a blouse with his purse slung over his shoulder, looking very 9–5. I loved seeing him coming down the street because wow! That man must have had the most courage in the world to walk through my neighborhood dressed like that. The few times we exchanged words, he was sweet as could be, but my dad called him a punk and told me to avoid him.

Interesting, isn't it, how someone sensitive and susceptible to prejudice and bigotry could turn around and deliver a good dose of it themselves? It's important to note here that my father has always loved and respected me unconditionally, and he has extended that love and respect to my partner. He's proof that you don't always need formal DEI training to evolve and change. In many instances, you just need love. Often people become better than their BS as soon as they realize that someone they care about or identify with falls into a category they've traditionally been biased against. As you'll see, many of the exercises in this book are designed to help speed that realization up, as well as help you see that the pool of people you can identify with is much wider and deeper than you probably imagined.

THINK BACK

Note: it will be important to answer all the questions in this book in writing. Writing down our thoughts and observations helps crystallize them in our minds and makes it harder to deny realizations that make us uncomfortable. It also gives us a permanent record, which is not only useful for when memory fails, but also good to have to look back on once we've evolved or made progress and want to see how far we've come or how much has changed.

- Which family members influenced your life when you were growing up?

- Was your family homogenous, or were some or many members different in some way from most of you?

- What did these family members say about people of different races, religion, sexual orientation, politics or gender identity, or disabilities, especially in private? How did their statements align with your internal belief system, or did what they taught you shape your belief system?

- Who was invited into your home to socialize and share meals? In whose homes were you invited?

- Did your family members show much interest in cultures different from yours? If they went out to eat, did they stick to their own culinary traditions or ones they were comfortable with, or did they sometimes like to try something new and unfamiliar?

Ring #2: Religion

Where did my family get its deep prejudice against homosexuals, even though few of them had ever even interacted with a gay person (to their knowledge)? Our whole lives, we heard the message loud and clear from the pulpit every Sunday: homosexuals were going to hell. So was anyone who didn't practice our Pentecostal denomination of Christianity, Church of God in Christ. Only a Jezebel wore makeup, pants, or jewelry. Even the wrong haircut could diminish you in God's eyes. I grew up thinking God was pretty boring and mean, but for a long time I wasn't willing to test Him, especially because the pastor of our church, the emissary of these dire warnings, was my grandfather.

He died a month after I graduated from high school, so I never learned what would have happened if he'd known his granddaughter was bisexual. When I signed a letter of intent to play basketball at Kansas State University, my favorite cousin, Carol, who was a former Wildcat, came home for a visit. A few days later, I discovered that this was a special trip to tell me something before I got to campus: she was gay, and she had a girlfriend. With tears in her eyes, she said she was telling me ahead of time so she didn't embarrass me. I couldn't blame Carol for being cautious—our families and the town we grew up in were close-minded in that regard. My mother was one of the few people Carol could talk to, and even Mom had to pray her way toward coming to terms with it. The people who raised and shaped me were loving, but my grandfather wasn't the only one with strict, closed religious beliefs. Still, I was horrified that she'd think I would ever reject her. "I love you," I told her. "You could never embarrass me."

Once I got to college and started recognizing that I, too, might be gay or bisexual, I understood Carol's fears even more. Grandpa was gone, but Ola Mae was still around, and I wasn't sure I could bear her disapproval. One day at KFC over a box of chicken tenders and a two-piece chicken combo—all white meat, Grandma's favorite—I casually brought up Carol and the family drama to see how she'd react. On the outside I was calm, but I could barely breathe. Grandma took her time with a few fries before saying thoughtfully that if people didn't like what Carol was doing, they should just pray for her and mind their own business. "She'll always be a good person." To this day, I don't know if she suspected anything about me; it would be another 10 years before I got comfortable admitting I wanted to be with women, and she had passed by then. Everyone always said she let me get away with things no one else would. But of this I am sure: whatever she thought about the way I lived my life, she loved me enough that she'd never have let her religious beliefs get between us.

THINK BACK

- What did your religious instructors or leaders teach you about gender roles or sexual orientation? How did it make you feel at the time?

- How did these lessons affect your behavior, or your career and romantic choices, later in life?

- Were you allowed to explore and participate in faith-based organizations outside of the one your family chose for you? If so, how did those differ?

- What discussions if any were you allowed to have with your church leaders when your opinion differed from what was taught?

- Who held positions of authority in your house of worship?

Ring #3: Peers and Friends

Sapulpa was a small town, numbering maybe 25,000 people, and of that total, only about a thousand were Black. Living on the Black side of town, however, ensured that my peers and I had a built-in community as we grew up. Then in middle school, my mom moved us from the Black side of town to the white side of town. I hated it. I missed the camaraderie, the barbecue grills, and seeing people playing pickup basketball at every open court in the neighborhood. I missed knowing every person I passed on the street. I resented having to watch how I spoke on my own block. Everyone speaks differently with friends than they do with family, and I had learned a long time ago that I had to speak differently—less Black—around my white friends than I did with my Black friends. But now that I no longer lived in a Black neighborhood, I had to watch my speech and behavior the minute I opened my front door.

I hung out with a pretty good crowd, but like most kids growing up in small towns where there isn't much to do, we often had to make our own fun. And there was fun that white kids could get up to that we Black kids knew we couldn't, because we'd pay a different consequence if we got caught. For example, the most country of pastimes, cow tipping. I know this sounds country AF, but here's how it worked: a carful of kids is moving along, and suddenly the driver pulls over to the side of a field where he's spotted a bunch of bovines dozing on their feet, as is natural. Everyone knows what to do. The white kids spill out of the car and start tipping the animals over. The Black kid—me—stays behind in the car as lookout. There was no way in hell I was taking the risk of planting my feet in a giant cow patty, putting my hands all over a huge, smelly animal, or getting caught messing with a white farmer's livelihood. The same thing went for certain parts of town. My white friends could go anywhere without question. I knew there were areas and surrounding small towns that weren't safe for me and those who looked like me.

At least I was able to continue attending my old school with my friends. Black people weren't numerous there, but at least we could look across a room and see someone else who looked like us. Not like my close friend Jerome, who lived in an even smaller town outside Sapulpa, where he was literally the only Black kid in school. He'd been adopted by a white lady and lived his whole life there. We met when he took a job working at a grocery store with some of my friends. He loved hanging out with us and going to our social events. Like many Black boys living in majority-white communities, sports gave him a place where he could belong, and he was a star player in every sport. I wasn't allowed to go to his games, because of the town he lived in, but one day I decided sneak off to accompany his girlfriend, Nicole. That was when I got a glimpse of why Jerome took such solace in the presence of a Black peer group. As the score tightened and tensions rose, people started calling racial epithets from the bleachers. There were only three Black people in the room: me, Nicole, and Jerome on the court. The mood of the crowd started darkening, and I was suddenly sorry Nicole and I hadn't thought to sit closer to an exit instead of the middle of the crowd. What if I had to call my daddy to get us out of there? What was the crowd going to do to Jerome? No one who was supposed to be on Jerome's side—not his teammates, not his coach—reacted to the taunts. I'd find out later that Jerome could hear everything that was going on, but he wasn't fazed. He was used to it. He'd had racial epithets carved into his locker. He'd had girls he liked tell him they couldn't go out with him because their parents wouldn't approve. This was nothing new. He made it out of there and grew up to become successful with a beautiful family. But though he was handsome as hell, he confessed to me that he always felt ugly. The years of being an oddity and a target in small-town Oklahoma had made their mark. Whatever racial or social issues my friends and I had to deal with, at least we'd had each other to lean on. Jerome had gone it alone.

THINK BACK

- Who did you play with as a child?
- Who did you hang out with as a teenager?
- How did these people look? What kind of homes did they live in? Did they have two parents or just one? Did anyone have two moms or two dads?
- If they were aware of the news or pop culture, what did they have to say?

Ring #4: Schools or Government

Schools and politics have always been closely inter-twined, from desegregation and what textbooks to adopt, to how to discuss racism in history and social studies class or whether to broach the subject at all. Aside from ninth grade when my Black history teacher, Mrs. Shirley Nero, sparked my interest in "real" Black history because she taught beyond what was printed in the textbook, my whole child-hood I learned almost exclusively about white historical figures, white authors, white innovators, and white cultural influences. Slavery was condensed to a page or two in our history books. The only positive information we got about Black people was limited to a select few Black heroes like Frederick Douglass, Harriet Tubman, Sojourner Truth, and MLK Jr. During Black History month, the Black kids would put on a show for the entire school but the other eleven months of the year, our classroom texts and discussions cen-tered on the accomplishments of white folk. Until finally, in world history class, we got to the unit on the Egyptians. Man, they were cool. Our teacher brought up Cleopatra, mentioning that she was supposed to be the most beautiful woman in the world at that time. My best friend threw up her hand. "Cleopatra was Black!" she announced excitedly. Well, that didn't go over so well. But my friend insisted. Egypt was on the African continent, and Egyptians were POC; obviously the most beautiful woman in the world during the 1st century BCE had to be Black. There ensued a hot debate over whether the Egyptians could really be con-sidered POC, with some people visibly uncomfortable that an icon like Cleopatra could be a woman of color. All I kept thinking was, the only time we talk about Black people in class is in relation to the horrors of slavery or the battle over civil rights. We finally get a beautiful queen, and you can't even let us have that without a fight? Meanwhile, in English class we were reading *Huckleberry Finn* and *To Kill a Mockingbird* out loud, and every time the N-word showed up, the teacher would give us Black kids the option of going out to the hallway so we didn't have to hear it. Somehow, the idea of just not saying the word ever again never came up. From then on, whenever I had a chance to choose my own research topic, no matter the class, I chose a Black person or a Black issue. I was going to take every opportunity to show the world that Black people had not only sweated and bled for this country, but contributed their intellect, innovation, passion, and creativity to our progress and entire body of knowledge. Can you imagine what it felt like as a young adult to realize that every year, K–12, I'd learned that Thomas Edison invented the light bulb, but it was never considered important to mention that a self-educated Black man, Lewis Latimer, devised the crucial improvement that extended the bulb's life, upgraded its efficiency, and enabled its use for lighting streets and homes? The fact that no one criticized the way marginalized students were taught about slavery or what they endured while reading racist literature or how history was always taught from the perspective of the victor further indicates why we need to assess our BS. Kids are resilient. They can handle the truth as shown by how marginalized kids have had to handle the lies and omissions in their education.

Our lives, and therefore our biases, are directly affected by government entities and legislators, especially at the local level, whether we choose to "do politics" or not. Kids who grow up in a state where doctors are forbidden to treat trans children with gender-affirming care will find their ability to comfortably navigate daily interactions with trans people stunted once they reach adulthood or move to a locale where trans kids are acknowledged and their mental health prioritized. Students who live in districts that ban books or even class discussions about sexual violence, LGBTQ+ issues, or non-white-centered history and racial tensions will have a limited understanding of the real world as they enter adulthood. Diverse people of any kind living in homogenous communities often struggle to be heard or gain representation, leading the dominant electorate to consider their issues as negligible, if they're considered at all. At a conference in San Diego, a white woman thanked me for my speech, adding that she'd recently moved to Texas. She said, "I'm a white woman struggling to live in Texas. How in the hell do you as a Black woman live in Oklahoma?" It's a question that I sometimes struggle to answer, but one powerful reason is that there are some amazing people in Oklahoma who want to see it become better.

THINK BACK

- Have your elected representatives always looked like you and championed issues you cared about? Did they talk about the opposing party or other constituents with respect, or lean in to inflammatory, insulting rhetoric? Did your friends or family members repeat their reps' talking points as dogma, or was there room for healthy debate, questions, and pushback?

- Did you notice any difference in the way school administrators treated boys and girls, or white children and other children?

Were standards, expectations, and discipline applied equally? If you're still friends with people who were part of that peer group when they were kids, do they remember school the same way you do?

- In K–12, did you have a diverse population of teachers? Did any identify as Latino, and did they teach a subject that wasn't Spanish?

- What were your school traditions? Do any strike you as questionable or outdated now?

- If you attended college, what kind was it? Why did you choose it? Who was there? When you looked around, who did you see? How did people talk about others? How did they talk about issues?

Ring #5: Mass Media

When I was about nine years old, my parents took our family on a road trip to Alabama. I loved visiting friends and family, but if I could have spent the entire time in front of the TV or in the car listening to the radio, that would have been fine with me. In Alabama, there were Black people on TV selling products to and for Black people! There was an ad featuring little Black girls playing with Black dolls! It's hard to stress how exciting and eye-opening it was to enter a world where people like me were a regular, frequent part of the media landscape. We never saw ourselves on screen. Until then, I had to glue myself to MTV and VH1 to make sure I didn't miss the one or two times per day they'd play Michael Jackson's "Billie

Jean" among the hourly rotations of Rod Stewart and Iron Maiden; it wasn't until 1984 we'd see any rap artists (Run DMC's "Rock Box"). The only families that looked anything like mine on TV were seen on *Good Times* and *The Jeffersons*, and we were neither as poor as the former nor anywhere as rich as the latter. To give you an idea of how much the media informs our perceptions, whenever I'd go to white friends' homes, I'd sneak a peek in the master bedroom to see if their parents had one bed like my folks, or if they slept in twin beds divided by a lamp and nightstand like the white couples in *Leave It to Beaver* and *I Love Lucy*, which I watched on reruns.

For many years, the media told me that the stories of Black people's lives weren't particularly interesting to the majority of the country. I learned that our music wasn't appealing to the mainstream until it was appropriated by white performers. When we were depicted on screen, in the news or entertainment, our characters were usually barely scraping by and frequently criminals, and if we had money, it was often because we were criminals (until the culturally earthshattering appearance of *The Cosby Show*). With a few exceptions, the message was reinforced over and over that white people were going to have a negative perception of me, and that I'd have to work five times as hard to get half as much.

This is one of those instances where the current news is bright. Today I can turn on the TV and see shows featuring people that look like me everywhere, not just BET. In fact, UCLA's 2021 Hollywood Diversity Report, spanning the 2019–2020 television season, reported that for the first time since it began collecting data, at 43.4 percent, the percentage of scripted roles played by POC was higher than the overall percentage of POC living in the U.S., though

Asian American, Latino, and Native American performers were still severely underrepresented.[3] In 2022, *Ms. Marvel*, featuring a mosque-attending Muslim teenager juggling superhero powers and the expectations of her Pakistani parents in Jersey City, became the highest scoring Marvel Comics Universe Disney+ series ever.[4] At the movies, almost 30 percent of films had levels of 50 percent or more of cast diversity across race and gender, a record. The films written and directed by women and POC had the highest levels of diversity, though they also tended to receive significantly less funding than their white, male peers, which limited their reach.[5] In 2022, Universal Pictures released the first mainstream, entirely LGBTQ+ romcom, *Bros*. The book publishing industry, too, is making efforts to diversify its predominantly white editorial workforce and release more books of all kinds by authors of color, even launching new imprints dedicated to publishing diverse books.[6] So people have many more options to see themselves in storylines and characters than ever before, and the media is recognizing that the mainstream is increasingly interested in seeing the world through perspectives beyond the "white gaze." But there will always be room for improvement until our mass media reflects the kaleidoscopic variety of its consumers. And the makeup of the people who decide what news to report and how to report it is still overwhelmingly homogenous. Data collected in February 2021 for a Reuters Institute report on the levels of diversity in editorial leadership at the top ten offline and online news outlets in markets across the world revealed a total of three non-white top editors in the U.S. sample.[7]

THINK BACK

- When you were growing up, what television shows did your family members regularly watch? What did you watch? What movies did you go see?

- What music did your family like to listen to? Do you remember questioning any of the lyrics? Do you remember hearing any judgment about other types of music?

- If you're white, did any of the books you read or that were popular among your peers feature protagonists who didn't look or sound like you?

- What did your family members have to say about the news and cultural issues?

THE RECKONING

So what do the results of this deep dive into the past reveal? Individual results will vary, but I can say for sure that one takeaway is that people are complicated, even the ones we admire most. And we can still love those complicated people, flaws and all, just as we want others to love us in spite of our imperfections. We don't conduct this exercise with the purpose of finding reasons to criticize the people we care about, or to poison our good memories. We do it for the same reason we always have to analyze the past from every angle, not just from the one that makes us feel or look good: because we can't fix problems if we're not even willing to acknowledge them, and we can't move forward if we don't know where we've been. Of course there's no guarantee that just because you grew up steeped in other people's BS automatically means you've absorbed it too, but the stats aren't in your favor. For example, babies as young as three months have been shown to prefer faces of their own race, and at six months show a preference for individuals who speak their own language.[8] That doesn't mean babies are racist. Not one bit. What it does mean is that no one is color blind, and, depending on what information we incorporate into our innate awareness of difference, it's easy to develop full-blown bias. Research also indicates that it's not our families' most virulent biases that affect us most; parents' subtle prejudices and "automatic behaviors and educational actions" may have an even stronger impact on their young children than any explicit prejudice.[9] Read that sentence again! It's imperative that we become better than our BS if we want our children to grow into adults who are not part of the problem, but rather immersed in the solution.

Look, you can't change the past. You can't control where your parents raised you, either, or where you went to school, and you can't do anything about the choices you made that have gotten you here. But you can do something about what happens next. With your new awareness, you can take a hard look at your environment and social circles, and where necessary start to diversify so any BS you do have will dissolve with exposure to different perspectives and experiences, and you'll be less likely to bring it with you into your workplace. Of course, because I'm a diversity expert who's immersed in the BS and preaches this every day, I've already done this and am perfectly positioned to model for you the kind of richly diverse personal life that helps prime us to improve our attitudes and interactions in the workplace.

Ahem.

Okay, so that's what I thought was true when I started writing this chapter. Yet when I took my own advice to heart and actually started taking a good, hard look at my world, I discovered I had as much work to do as anyone.

TAKE STOCK

We just examined the biasphere in which we grew up to get to the heart of our BS. We now have to examine the biasphere we live in today to see how we keep perpetuating it.

- Who are the five people you speak and/or visit with the most outside your family of origin? In what ways do these people align with your race, gender, religion, sexual orientation, or political affiliation? In what ways do they differ?

    (You'll notice that we skipped Ring #1, Family. That's because we don't get to choose our families of origin, so the homogeneity or diversity of the first ring of our biasphere isn't within our control. Even if you consider a sibling or cousin to be your best friend, for the purposes of this exercise I want you to think about the ones you have chosen to be in your life and not those who were born into it. Later, however, we'll discuss ways to start broadening the perspectives of immediate family members—blood and chosen—who may still be entrenched in the BS you or your partner were raised with.)

What differing perspectives do you hold? Do you avoid discussing them?

- If you participate in organized religion or any type of communal worship, where do you attend services? What does your religious or spiritual community look like? Does it embrace or reject an "us" vs. "them"?

- If you went to college, where did you go? Did you take any classes that took you outside your comfort zone or that were complete departures from the things you believed to be true? Did the college experience help you grow? Who did you socialize with there? Are you still connected to any of those friends? In what ways do these people align with your race, gender, religion, sexual orientation, or political affiliation? In what ways do they differ?

- If you went to trade school or entered the workforce right after high school, how did you continue to educate yourself? Did you ever take a class or read material that took you outside your comfort zone? Are you still connected to any of the people you met in those early days of your training or career? In what ways do these people align with your race, gender, religion, sexual orientation, or political affiliation? In what ways do they differ?

- If you have children, where do you send them to school? What are the racial, religious, and socioeconomic demographics? Are diverse books prominently displayed in the library? Would you consider a school that draws kids from all over the city, or are you happy for your kids to go to school with only kids from your own neighborhood? Have families fought efforts to change school boundaries that would socioeconomically integrate schools better so that more kids can benefit from neighborhood wealth and academic resources? Does the school highlight other cultures, for example by setting up an *ofrenda* on Día de los Muertos, or expose kids to information about all the winter holidays that take place around the world besides Christmas? Is it a place that welcomes the chance to explore history all year long from multiple perspectives, not just through a white lens or from the "winner's" perspective? Does it share the stories of people who have traditionally not been included or welcomed in the historical narrative?

- How aware are you of the role government or politics play in your life? What politicians or public servants do you support or admire? Do they all match your race, gender, religion, sexual orientation, or political affiliation? Are there some that don't?

- What type of TV shows or movies do you watch? What type of music do you listen to? What books do you read, or websites and blogs do you follow? Are there any whose audience is not traditionally someone of your race, gender, ethnicity, sexuality, or culture?

- Where do you consume news and media? Do you follow any channels, social media profiles, or online communities whose target audience does not generally align with your political leanings?

So, when I asked myself these questions, how did I do? It was easy to list the top five friends closest to me. They are my speaking manager, Shannyn; my friend delmetria (who spells her name in lowercase letters, same as bell hooks); my friend Ron; my partner, Arielle; and then I lumped a group of seven girlfriends I've known my whole life—we call ourselves the SapTown homies—into one entity, because few days go by when we don't all chat and text. Then I made a chart to mark their race, gender, religion, sexual orientation, and political affiliation so I could see where we were the same and where we differed.

Name	Race	Gender	Religion	Sexual Orientation	Political Affiliation
Shannyn		x			x
delmetria	x	x	x	x	x
Ron	x		x-ish		
Arielle	x	x	x	x	x
SapTown Homies	x	x	x-ish		x

One white person, and one man who was also the only person with whom I don't share a political affiliation. I was surprised. When I think of my friend group—the people whose homes I'm invited to, who are invited into mine, who I meet for social gatherings and holidays—I picture a lot of white and brown faces, some of whom I consider family. But when I forced myself to be honest about the people I speak to and hang with the most, none of them made the list. I love Shannyn, and we have a great time chatting on the phone (she lives in Canada), but would we talk as much as we do if we hadn't been in business together for five years? I could think of at least two white friends who had reached out to me over the years to get together, and I'd consistently put them off, even though I love hanging out with them. A Hispanic friend I do see more often lately has been the one to instigate our get-togethers. My reasons for being unavailable were legit: I was busy, I was going through a tough time, or I didn't have the energy after a heavy traveling schedule. I just don't get to see my friends a lot, period, because of my schedule and business commitments, but doing this exercise made me realize that when my Black friends reached out, I usually made time for them, and on the rare occasions that I instigated an outing, they were the ones I called. I was disappointed to see this because it proves I'm missing out on connecting with people I really care about and who enrich my life. I plan to be better than my BS and reconnect because these folks are so dope!

My answers to the remaining questions didn't look particularly diverse either.

School: Like many Black kids, I was inspired to attend a historically Black college or university (HBCU) after watching *A Different World*, the TV show that chronicled the on-again, off-again romance between bougie Whitley Gilbert and nerdy Dwayne Wayne at the fictional HBCU Hillman College. Unfortunately, HBCUs have been historically underfunded and lack the wealthy alumni who can make monster donations and set up endowments, so though several recruited me, none were able to offer me full basketball scholarships to attend as other schools, which is how I landed at Northern Oklahoma college, then Kansas State University.

Government and politics: Surprise! You're surely not shocked to learn that I lean pretty liberal. Overall, aside from my religious family members, with most of my friends sharing my political views, and the work that I do, my world is mostly full of liberal folk. Also thanks to my work, however, I'm exposed to the thinking of many conservatives, and I do have associates who are more conservative than I am. How am I to empathize with people who struggle to accept and adapt to rapidly changing cultural mores and social norms if I isolate myself from them? If I'm really going to walk the walk of Radical Acceptance, I should be able to develop friendships with conservatives. Then there is Ron, my homeboy bestie. He is a Black Republican. He's an amazing, intelligent guy who has been there for me and stepped up for so many others in ways that would make your jaw drop, without expectations of reward or public acknowledgment. So on the days when we "get into it" and he tries to explain the business case for his position on legislative issues and his voting record, I grit my teeth and force myself to listen. Because sometimes, if I can hold on long enough, I'll start to see his point. I won't agree with it, but I'll have an inkling of understanding for why he sees things the way he does. It's not easy to sit in that space, but our friendship is worth it. He will hear me out as well. There have been times we've had heated discussions in which we've had to agree to disagree. There have been other times when I've shared a thought that has led him to cock his big head to the side, look directly at me, and say, "Well, that sounds mighty Republican of you."

Media: TV shows I watch: *90-Day Fiancé*, *The Profit*, *Shark Tank*

Movies: I'm always drawn to movies with Black characters and Black culture, LGBTQ+ characters or issues, and superheroes. I'll also admit that I'm always up for a good Lifetime movie.

Music: R&B, old school hip-hop, smooth jazz. Some country music also gets my toes tapping.

Books: Novels by Black authors, business, spiritual, anything by James Patterson

News: *Good Morning America, The New York Times, Daily Skimm*, CNBC, and every once in a while, FOX News (yes, I said it. It's my attempt to hear all sides of the issues).

My answers to my own questionnaire were eye-opening. With a few exceptions, I could see that my world wasn't very inclusive at all. It's essentially Black. As much as I work with diverse groups of people every single day and consume different perspectives, that work is not translating to better diversity outside of work hours.

Why would this be? The answer is likely different for me than it would be for someone who's a member of a dominant culture. In the U.S. and especially in my home state of Oklahoma, BIPOC, LGBTQ+ people, and non-Christians don't have any choice but to insert themselves into straight, white, Christian culture. We're used to it. If you want to be successful in business, the arts, academia, if you want upward mobility, you have to work to fit in and make the dominant culture accept and welcome you. Before we had the ability to stream curated news, music, books, or programs 24/7, BIPOC had access to only select few channels, programs, stations, or subscriptions that spoke to their identity or experiences, whereas cis white Christians could see themselves reflected almost anywhere they looked as soon as they woke up every day. And until extremely recently, anyone outside that dominant group had to actively seek out a biasphere beyond their immediate family and religion to find themselves represented or others who might understand where they're coming from. For example, at the end of 2020, *The New York Times* examined a select list of widely read—meaning easily accessible in libraries and available in digital form—English-language fiction books published between 1950 and 2018. Ninety-five percent were written by white authors.[10] Earlier in the year, a Twitter campaign revealed that award-winning authors of color were often paid a quarter of the advances offered first-time white authors.[11] We can surmise how that statistic could influence the number of POC who'd even bother to try to get their work published in the mainstream, which would then limit the number of books available to POC looking for novels that speak to their experiences and culture. Even when industries try to change the landscape, as many including publishing are doing now, it takes time, and in the meantime it's hard to break years of mindset and habit.

Regardless, I wasn't happy to see that I'd cultivated a homogenous biasphere. Not that what I was seeing was "bad." In fact, it's important to understand that no matter how your answers look, none of the results will be in and of themselves "bad." No one should ever apologize for where they come from or be ashamed to love their family members. I would never ask you to freeze loved ones out or drop friendships, no matter what this exercise revealed, unless you believed their presence in your life was harmful in some way. There's nothing better than spending time with people you can speak with in shorthand or slang because they share your background, vocabulary, and reference points to the extent they can probably finish your sentences. That depth of connection and understanding is precious and valuable. The problem with a homogenous biasphere isn't that it's homogenous. It's that it's limiting.

If I see work, religion, society, love, and marriage through the exact same lens wherever I go, that has to affect how I respond to someone who crosses my path at work who is totally the opposite of everything I thought I knew. I may believe I'm treating people equally, but how would I know when I lack meaningful relationships with anyone not like me? Who would tell me—who would even notice—if my biases led me to inadvertently snub or hurt someone who didn't have the power to tell me themselves? If I were a company manager and in a position to grant professional opportunities, wouldn't it be possible that my BS could cause me to unconsciously overlook them for a full and fair consideration? Am I sure that I'm fully listening to these people when they speak, or is it possible I'm dismissing or only partially hearing their ideas or concerns?

If you can look down at your piece of paper and see that you're getting all of your information and perspective about the world from one angle, it's highly likely that your mind isn't as open to varying perspectives as you think it is. And on an even bigger scale, if your goal is to produce better products and services, and reach bigger markets, it can only help to get a broader sense of how different people operate within the world and interpret their experiences. To do that, you have to dive into other ecosystems. And you have to do it intentionally.

BREAK DOWN YOUR BS

The first step in breaking down your BS is to dive into a new biasphere, one rich with new information and points of view. As a starting point, I've included a list of books, podcasts, websites, and other resources at the end of this book that can help.

As you consume this new content and educate yourself, you may want to start to join the conversation, or you may find you have questions whose answers aren't addressed in any of the resources above. Even if there are people in your orbit you could turn to for answers, I'm going to ask you to hold off. There will come a time when you should reach out to the people you know, if only casually, who might have insight into some of these issues, but we're not there yet. In the meantime, social media, websites, and other online forums can be great places to see conversations on all sorts of topics happening in real time. For example, Reddit is full of Q&As on every topic you can think of.

RADICAL ACT

Find people having interesting conversations about current events that offer insight into perspectives that were previously unfamiliar to you and start following them. Don't add your voice. Just watch, read, and learn.

Social media can be a cesspool of insults and vile behavior, but it is also a place where if you choose wisely where to look, you can find intelligent people productively challenging and informing each other.

Analyzing your biasphere and identifying your BS raises your unconscious bias to the conscious level. If you don't like what you discover, don't blame or judge yourself, not because bias isn't problematic, but because getting caught up in your feelings is a distraction. What matters is what you're going to do about it, because once you can see your BS, you're also quickly going to see that it's been running your life for a long time and warping your ability to gauge reality. Congratulations. Fortunately, the next chapter will show you there are ways to undo all that shit too.

CHAPTER 3

BIAS → FEAR

The Curse of Scarcity Mentality

In 2018, one of my new tech clients, a huge cybersecurity firm, announced they were committing to a DEI initiative that would ensure at least 50 percent of their employees would be women, people of color, or LGBTQ+ by the year 2020. I cheered their audacious goal, but I also warned them to be careful about how they explained their plans to the group of mostly young white guys that made up their employee base. It was possible that news of this new plan would freak them out. Not a problem, the CPO (chief people officer) assured me. This was tech, and the company was full of the most educated, open-minded, come-as-you-are folks you'd ever want to meet. Plus, one of their leaders was Black!

A few months later, the CPO called me back. Some of the company's employees had turned into jackasses, and others were worried that the company's focus on diversity and inclusion would leave out white men. I wasn't surprised. See, what company execs failed to appreciate is that anyone accustomed to living at the top of the heap also frequently lives in a zero-sum world in which there are only winners and losers. What this means is that when you say to a group of white dudes that from now on, you're going to actively start recruiting from a more diverse pool of candidates, what many actually hear is that in a world of limited resources, "If you hire them, there will be fewer jobs for us."

That fearful thinking pattern isn't limited to this admirable company, or just the tech industry. At every company that brings me in for consulting, I send out an anonymous survey asking employees what they fear will happen when their company adopts a DEI program. With over 100,000 responses in hand, the prevailing answer is unambiguous: they fear that "undeserving" diverse individuals will take their jobs, or that they'll lose opportunities for promotions because they don't qualify as diverse.

But how rational is that fear? Do we really live in a world of limited resources, or have we just been told we do? Is there a documented wave of white, straight, or male employees getting shoved out of their jobs or denied opportunities to build thriving careers?

Let's look at the facts as of the writing of this book:

- 92.6 percent of Fortune 500 CEOs are white;[1] 90 percent are white men.[2]

- 79.4 percent of Fortune 100 board directors are white men.[3]

- 61.7 percent of Fortune 500 board directors are white men.[4]

- Improvement to overall diversity of boards and CEO suites was mostly made by the addition of white women.[5]

- Approximately 1 in 5 C-suite executives is a woman; only 1 in 25 is a woman of color[6.]

- Men hold 62 percent of all first-rung manager-level positions, leaving fewer women in the running for higher-level promotions and hires.[7]

- Whites only make up about 62 percent of college students, yet they receive nearly 75 percent of all private scholarships.[8]

- Less than 1 percent of Fortune 500 board directors are openly LGBTQ+.[9]

- There are only four openly gay Fortune 500 CEOs.[10]

WHAT'S SCARCITY MENTALITY?

The fear that employees will be pushed out of their jobs when a company commits to diversity, inclusion, and equity is far greater than any evidence that it actually happens. It's residue from your biasphere, and if you're not careful, it can lead to a special byproduct of fear that keeps you from living on your own terms as well as warp your ability to gauge reality. It's called *scarcity mentality*, a term coined by Stephen Covey. Scarcity mentality is the mindset that if others get more, we will necessarily have less, i.e., zero-sum thinking. Most of us are pretty cool when we feel secure, but it's not uncommon for us to lose our shit as soon as we sense that someone else has access to favors, attention, information, or status we don't or can't have. When we feel threatened, we can become condescending, resentful, dismissive, grasping, and mean. We start thinking in terms of "us" vs. "them," and resist ideas and solutions if we believe they benefit others more than ourselves.

In short, scarcity mentality makes us behave like assholes and bullies. It exists everywhere, but in companies that try to introduce DEI without the right game plan, it can be especially rampant and poisonous.

Maybe you don't think you suffer from scarcity mentality. Let's find out. Answer these questions:

- Do you believe there are enough resources in the world for everyone to meet their own needs?

  People in rich, Western countries generally agree that yes, there are.

  Let's narrow that question further:

- Do you believe there are enough resources within your company for everyone to earn a living wage?

  It's easy to believe there is enough to go around when you perceive some distance between yourself and the rest of the world. It gets a little harder when that distance shrinks, doesn't it?

- Do you believe your department recruits enough diverse people?

- Are there enough opportunities for promotions that you don't or won't feel left out when a diverse colleague receives one ahead of you?

- Do you believe in pay equity for women and POC?

When pressed, many people who generally feel secure in their place in the world at large have to admit that when it comes to the workplace, they're harboring some Hunger Games–level fear.

If that's you, you're fearing a made-up problem. Scarcity mentality is rooted in false assumptions and evaluations about how the world works. For example, a common concern about DEI initiatives is that work quality will go down if companies make the effort to hire more women or POC. Meanwhile, in reality, companies that embrace DEI consistently show increased profits, innovation, and growth. In addition, I challenge anyone to find a woman or POC who would apply for or accept a job offer for a position they didn't feel qualified to do. Who would want to set themselves up for failure like that? The idea that anyone would be happy to be handed a job for no reason other than their gender or the color of their skin is as offensive as someone assuming you got your job because you're related to someone at the company or had a connection who could pull strings and not because you have any talent or skill. All anyone has ever asked for is a fair chance to compete, prove themselves, and reach for a good quality of life.

Yet despite employment discrimination being illegal on paper, it's constantly being perpetuated, even if unintentionally. Studies have confirmed again and again[11] that employers hire people they like, which is frequently predicated on the sharing of common attributes, backgrounds, and education, or an assessment of who will "fit" into company culture. If you look at the stats above, you can see who historically and statistically has been in a position to make hiring decisions and establish culture. And if employers prefer to hire candidates who look, sound, and share the same background as they do, clearly it's white people, and men in particular, who have had an unearned advantage all along. If you've been the beneficiary of this system (hint: if you've never had to think about it, you've likely been the beneficiary), it's understandable that these social and cultural shifts might feel a little disorienting or even painful. That pain or disorientation you might be feeling for the first time, however, is the pain and disorientation that millions of people have suffered and documented for generations. The only difference is that before, you could ignore the problem because it wasn't yours. That, in essence, is privilege.

THE P-WORD

Until now, I've avoided using that word because I know how many people receive it. They've been primed to believe that to be told they have unearned privilege minimizes how hard they worked to get anywhere in life, or dismisses their own hardships such as poverty, illness, or family instability. They've been told that someone who would point out their privilege is trying to undermine their success. But that's not how privilege works, and in my experience, the people who insist it is frequently have a vested interest in keeping as many people as possible planted firmly in a state of scarcity mentality.

I'll be the first to admit that I have benefited from certain unearned privileges. I was born to a loving, stable, two-parent home surrounded by family and friends who emotionally supported me and encouraged my dreams and goals. I grew up middle class, and was (as one of my good friends jokingly likes to remind me) one of the few Black student athletes in high school and college with health insurance. I have never worried about how I was going to eat, because even during the years I was building my business and money was extremely tight or non-existent, I could go eat at my mom's house or practically any of my relatives' homes. Being from a big family comes in handy for some things. They never knew that I didn't have money for food because they never asked why I was there. They opened their homes and refrigerators with love.

I didn't build that environment through hard work, but it undoubtedly gave me advantages as I moved through life that people without that kind of family network don't enjoy. I may have had to deal with other adversity, including discrimination and bias. For example, I had to make sure my hands were visible when I went shopping, and that I always asked for a bag and receipt at the store even for the smallest purchases, because I knew store employees and security guards would be watching me more closely, and be more likely to ask me for proof of purchase as I left the store, than they would a white person. But I never had to spend any emotional or mental energy doubting that my family had my back or wanted anything but the best for me. That's a huge psychological burden I never had to carry.

Someone with financial privilege can take certain educational or career risks because they know they'll eat the next month even if the risk doesn't pay off. Someone with ability privilege never has to think for a second about what kind of accommodations they need to arrange ahead of time before traveling, or attending a performance, or even using office space. If you have straight privilege, you never have to worry about attracting violence or ugly remarks for holding your partner's hand or showing other affection in public. If you have religious privilege, you will see your religious holidays represented in every retail establishment and on every website you visit, especially in December, and if you chose, you could easily avoid knowing a thing about other religious holiday traditions. Finally, if you have white privilege, it simply means that you can move through the world without giving any thought to your race. If you are white and grew up in the United States, you may have had a hardscrabble life, suffered trauma, overcome enormous obstacles, or been born or raised with many strikes against you, but the fact is, your race was not one of them. You didn't have to make a special effort to find entertainment that reflected your experience or values. You rarely have to wonder if you'll see someone who looks like you in your corporate workplace. You can safely assume that people will judge your work, talent, and accomplishments without being affected by any unconscious BS they've linked to people with your skin color because most of the time the people making hiring decisions look just like you. The advantages bestowed upon us by our privilege, white or otherwise, often aren't about what we have so much as what we have never had to worry about.

RADICAL ACCEPTANCE CURES SCARCITY MENTALITY

I get it. Even if you understand why you can't take for granted the economic opportunities previous generations who look like you enjoyed, and even if you agree that the recruiting and hiring disparities were long unfair toward BIPOC, it still sucks to feel like you might be sidelined for no other reason than your race or gender. This is where Radical Acceptance works its magic by showing you that correcting for unfair hiring and recruiting practices doesn't sideline you at all. Once you are armed with a clear understanding of your own unconscious biases, it's not threatening to examine how you might have benefited from policies that have kept BIPOC from climbing career ladders. It is what it is.

Here's the thing. If you've kept up to date with advancements in your industry, kept your networks fresh, and proven yourself an invaluable employee, you can likely feel confident that your job isn't in danger and that you're perfectly positioned to compete for the next job or promotion if you choose to go for it. The only thing that might have changed is that you might not automatically get that job or promotion. DEI doesn't tilt the playing field in anyone's direction, but rather takes bias out of the hiring process by broadening the candidate pool and prioritizing inclusion, which merely ensures that members of groups who've been overlooked for years finally get a fair chance to compete.

If you're feeling vulnerable at work, the problem isn't DEI. The problem lies in how most companies communicate DEI goals and benefits, and how they address, or fail to address, people's understandable concerns. Later in this book we'll go over how companies can improve their DEI rollout without scaring people into thinking their jobs are at risk, but right now we can tackle the most common worries that usually come up:

Myth #1: I'll get pushed out of my job so the company can replace me with a person of color or someone different from me.

The only risk you have of losing your job is if you do or say something inappropriate because you weren't able to get your BS under control. As we'll see later in Chapter 9,

DEI programs show companies how to expand their talent pipeline to improve their recruiting and hiring practices, not how to get rid of people.

Myth #2: Quotas mean I'll never get promoted again.

The goal with DEI isn't supposed to be about filling a certain number of positions with people who match your racial and gender checklist. When done correctly, it's about building a connected culture from the ground up, in which inclusion happens at every level of the company, from recruitment to retention. I've yet to work with a single company that has suddenly stopped promoting their white or male employees. If that were happening at any scale, we wouldn't see the stats listed at the beginning of this chapter.

Myth #3 "Equity" is code for "handout."

Three months after I moved into a new home, my sister had surgery on her Achilles tendon. It wasn't until I watched her struggle to get into my house with her post-surgery boot and crutches that I realized there were steep steps in front of almost every entryway, and that anyone with mobility issues would have a hard time entering my home. My sister's condition was temporary, but had it been permanent, you better believe I would have built a small ramp to make sure she could come visit any time she wanted. I wouldn't be giving her a handout; I would be making sure a person I valued wasn't shut out. It wouldn't have been a hardship for me, either. When change is important to you, you make it happen.

So it goes with equity. All equity means is that systems that may have been intentionally or unintentionally designed to favor one group over another have been leveled so that each individual has the opportunity to showcase the best of their skills and talents and is assured they will be fairly assessed. Equity is simply good management—making sure all employees have access to what they need to succeed. It can be a tall order. Yet if you have a talented employee who's hard of hearing, it's to your benefit to make sure they have access to closed captioning or a headset so they can perform at their best. If someone has poor eyesight, it's in your best interest to make sure they have text-to-speech assistance on your technology and websites. A young employee or someone with a nontraditional background might simply need a mentor to make sure they keep growing into their role and become your company's superstar. Not all companies can provide these supports, but it's something to aspire toward. Companies with this mindset are in a better position to win.

All that said, I'm not going to deny that there have been cases where people get pushed out of their jobs. You know who's most at risk? Older workers. You know why? It's not because of DEI. It's because when companies want to cut costs, they target higher-paying mid-level and upper-level jobs, replacing them with younger, less experienced workers who will cost them less in salaries and insurance. It's because when companies say they want "fresh" talent and require advanced degrees and familiarity with tech to fill a position, they've made demands that frequently exclude older workers who didn't need those prerequisites to start their careers and move up. Ageism's a bitch, and it's getting worse. In fact, in an AARP survey taken in 2020, 78 percent of older workers said they saw or experienced age discrimination in the workplace, up from 61 percent in 2018. That's the highest level ever recorded since AARP started asking the question in 2003.[12] And as

Phyllis Weiss Haserot astutely noted in an article published for *Thomson Reuters*, ageism isn't limited to older people. When young or new employees are condescended to as "kids," or Millennials are accused of being lazy and entitled, that's ageism. And just because ageism hasn't come for you yet doesn't mean it won't. "Age is not static, and bias can—and eventually will—affect people at any age."[13] A well-developed DEI initiative can work to curb our worst instincts, bad habits, and BS, and prepare everyone for a future of unlimited opportunity, productivity, and career longevity.

HOW DEI BENEFITS YOU!

Embracing Radical Acceptance improves your career prospects because it prompts you to do the introspective work that will make you a better leader and manager. Think of the process like a construction project to expand or improve your local highway—inconvenient and frustrating at times, but ultimately resulting in a road that helps everyone get where they want to go with greater ease. Progress can be messy, and change can be painful— unless you're willing to be part of the solution. By supporting new policies that ensure everyone has access to what they individually need to be successful, you'll be able to build a system where everyone, including you, wins. You can choose to let scarcity mentality fuel your anxiety, or you can choose an *abundance mentality*, another Stephen Covey term. In other words, instead of fearing what you might lose, consider what you could gain. And if it takes a little adjustment, that's okay! It wouldn't be the first time you adapted to something new. Depending on your age, you might have seen smoking sections, fax machines, and

Rolodexes disappear. You learned to text and Venmo. Ten years ago you didn't have a virtual assistant in your home, and you didn't shop curbside; today, you likely do. If you bought a new car in the last decade, you got used to blind spot monitors and maybe even self-parking. You are far more multiskilled and flexible than you realize.

Companies will always do what's best for their bottom line, which means they aren't in the habit of missing out on great talent. Someone with serious skills, like you, will always be in demand. It's just a matter of highlighting the unique value you have to offer any company in your industry. Adopting an abundance mentality is never a bad idea, but to catapult your career, pair it with a growth mentality. What skills can you learn that will make you even more valuable to your company? What areas of improvement are within your control? If you want to be a stronger, better competitor than anyone else, you have to put in the work. Scarcity mentality allows the world to decide how much is available to you. A growth mentality empowers you to decide how much you want.

The fact is, the changes we're talking about are happening, and they're going to happen faster and more frequently as the years progress. The 2020 census revealed that for the first time since we started tracking the demographics and social patterns of our country, the number of people who identify as white shrank. Whites who are non-Hispanic make up only 58 percent of our population now[14] and are projected to fall below 50 percent in the next 25 years.[15] The under-18 population, and the next generation of workers, is now majority people of color, and as John Della Volpe, director of polling at the Harvard Kennedy School's Institute of Politics, wrote in *Fight*, his examination of the evolution of Gen Z, "They will change

America more than growing up in America will change them."[16] You can be part of the solution now and help create a more welcoming environment, or you can be dragged into it, kicking and screaming, possibly enacting a self-fulfilling prophecy by saying or doing something inappropriate and facing consequences for it. The great thing is, if we put systems in place to create equity today, we won't have to keep having these conversations tomorrow, and it will soon feel like second nature.

What we do to the least of us will eventually happen to all of us. None of the changes DEI promotes result in overnight transformations, but we have to start somewhere. If we don't start taking steps to fix things now, we'll never stop dealing with this problem. Yet if we all work together to change the culture so that everyone feels valued and included at work, there will be a day when it is a nonissue, and no one ever has to worry about it anymore.

I once conducted a workshop with a huge conglomeration of U.S. stores, and when I asked people to anonymously tell me what they found challenging about embracing DEI, one of them wrote: "I'm so scared of Black people that I don't hire them in my stores." Bruh. And yet, I appreciated the honesty. It gave me a way to tie a direct link between someone's BS and the very real issues DEI was created to fix. Do I believe that this individual walks around saying terrible things to Black people? I don't. Yet this person's racism and prejudice surely manifests itself in a subtle, silent, yet profoundly damaging way. There's a high likelihood that this person who doesn't want to give Black people jobs is also the first to say that Black people don't want to work. If you're allowing your BS to keep you from hiring, promoting, or paying the same wages to a group of people, that's keeping them from their American

Dream. You are literally preventing others from building the same quality of life you take for granted. You expect them to fail, and then you make sure they do.

The thing that limits us the most is ourselves when we indulge in our BS and allow it to fuel suspicions, prejudices, and fear, or to keep people out based on nothing more than history and habit. You only think your BS is giving you accurate information because you've never been willing to look beyond your biasphere, but the world looks quite different once you step outside of it. In fact, it can force you to reconsider everything you thought was true. That reevaluation is what sets you irrevocably on your way to becoming better than your BS.

CHAPTER 4

REDEFINING NORMAL

For years, my grandmother worked as a maid for a white family in the small town where I grew up. Her boss owned a popular department store, so they were considered a good family to work for. When her boss's grandkids were in town, Grandma would sometimes bring me to work with her so I could play with them. They lived on the white side of town in a big house with a manicured lawn. Theirs was the first house I'd been to that had a piano. Normally, like most kids growing up in the early '80s, we played outside, but one day the kids and I found ourselves hanging out on the living room floor while Grandma worked somewhere else in the house. The kids' mother and grandmother sat on the couch, their knees at our eye level. The grown-ups were talking playfully with the kids, as grown-ups like to do, until one of them asked us all what we wanted to be when we grew up. The little boy piped up that he wanted to be a policeman. The white ladies clapped and cheered. The little girl said something, but by then my mind was spinning and I wasn't listening anymore, because I'd never thought about this question in my life. I didn't know what to say! I heard the white ladies clap and cheer again, and knew that it was now my turn to talk. I thought about my grandma, and how mostly everyone I knew thought she was the coolest lady around. She was known as the town baker and, as the wife of a minister, a first lady of the church. I opened my mouth and announced in a room full of white people that I wanted to be a maid, just like my grandma. The adults clapped and cheered my choice, just like they had the other kids', and I breathed a sigh of relief. *Cool*, I thought. I'd made a good decision.

Suddenly, my grandmother flew out from wherever she'd been listening. She wasn't known for being a strong disciplinarian, so when I saw her coming for me, I knew I was in trouble. "You will *never* be a maid!" she said, gripping my shoulders and shaking me until I looked straight into her eyes. "Do you think I'm doing this because I want to? I do this because I have to. You—you will go to college, become a teacher, or get a job working for the government." The clapping had stopped. The room stayed quiet.

When we climbed into her blue Chevy at the end of the day, Grandma remained visibly shaken. On our way home, she explained to me that she'd actually always wanted to be a nurse, but "they" wouldn't allow her. It wasn't the first time I'd heard about these mysterious "theys," but it would be a bit longer before I got the courage to ask her to identify them for me in the Walmart parking lot.

Let's break this down:

I wanted to be a maid because one of the people I loved most in the world was a maid. Not only that, all her sisters were maids, also working for families on the white side of town. Even though my dad was an airplane mechanic for a large international company and my mom worked for a well-known airline. I never went to work with them or heard them talk about their jobs much, so this was my normal.

The white people applauded my choice because my ambitions fell perfectly within the parameters they could envision for a little Black girl. That was their normal.

And then there was Grandma, who had bigger dreams for me than anyone in that room could conceive, and who knew the world had changed and that what had been normal for her generation, white or Black, would not be for mine. Even so, at every turn she made damn sure I not only lived up to, but surpassed standards established by people who did not look like her. She and my aunt spent a summer teaching me to read, write, and count to ensure that I'd be ahead in class out of concern "they" wouldn't teach me the same way "they" taught the white kids. She insisted that I look and behave impeccably in public, for fear "they" would think I hadn't been raised right. Her dreams for me included teaching, because that was a job for respectable women, or government work, because that meant lifelong stability. And of course, she assumed I'd be a wife, a mother, and a stout COGIC Christian. Because as much as the world had changed, that was still her normal, and she believed she'd be derelict in her grandma duties if she didn't make sure it was mine too.

Despite her vision and hopes for the future, Grandma was as much at the mercy of her biasphere as anyone else. That, y'all, is its power and purpose—to make sure that as we grow, we stick to belief systems that keep us thinking and behaving within the boundaries of what a select few decide is "normal." But WTF does "normal" even mean, especially when it changes so much? Not long before my grandmother tried to shake my teeth out in her boss's living room, the only women at the office were working in the steno pool, and all were young and white; companies used code words in their help-wanted ads or questioned an applicant's lineage to filter Jews out of the hiring process; and all men wore suits to the office and their hair short. Not long after, visible tattoos and multiple ear piercings would become acceptable for respectable professionals and tradespeople, not just punks and rebels, and full-time office workers would no longer be expected to leave their homes for work every day to get their jobs done. Yet, in the future, none of these examples will ever likely be considered "normal" to Generation Alpha, or the Divergents,[1] or whatever label eventually sticks to the babies being born today. They'll decide their own normal.

Each time another barrier for a previously marginalized group fell, or another clothing style relaxed, or another tradition curled up and died, people who liked things the way they were would fret and predict a disastrous lowering of the country's standards, prosperity, and productivity. And each time, we adjusted and moved on. Today, we find the more superficial of the old mores, like clothing styles, laughable, and we're horrified by the more serious ones like overt job discrimination. Yet to this day, in all these arenas our standards of "normal" continue to be set by the same select few who dictated all those laughable, horrifying old rules. It's important to understand the fear-based marketing job that got billions across generations to agree that life is usually best lived the way white, hetero people find most reassuring and comfortable. How'd they do it? By capitalizing on the primal human need to belong.

THE BIOLOGY OF BELONGING

"Belongingness," as psychologist Abraham Maslow called it,[2] falls smack in the middle of the pyramid that represents his human hierarchy of needs, subordinate only to the basic requirements of food and water, warmth, rest, and safety. Social scientists suggest that it's one of the fundamental drivers of our behavior,[3] because evolutionarily speaking, we're just not that far removed from our prehistoric ancestors roaming the tundra or savanna. In their world, to be ostracized—to be rejected, ignored, or excluded from the group—meant almost certain death. Which probably explains why, according to Dr. Matthew Lieberman and Dr. Naomi Eisenberger, being ostracized activates similar circuits in the brain as when we suffer a physical injury.[4] Experiments by Dr. Kipling Williams, a professor of psychological science at Purdue University, suggest that being ostracized for only short periods of time, by strangers, can register as pain.[5] It makes sense when you realize that for eons, being rejected from the group effectively blocked us from the resources necessary for our survival. Translated to the modern work world, those resources take the form of information, networks, moral support, and encouragement—everything you need for professional survival.

Belonging gives us psychological safety. It gives us confidence and comfort because we know we're not all alone. Maslow's hierarchy tells us that not having to worry about our basic physical and emotional needs liberates us to work toward fulfilling "self-actualization needs," whereby we just might have a shot at reaching the pinnacle of our potential and emotional growth. Once more, let's translate that to the work world. When we're no longer spending time and energy shoring up our "belongingness" to ensure our survival at work, we're motivated to unleash our creativity, test our boundaries, and take risks.

So if we're hardwired to strive for acceptance and connection, what happens when it's withheld? Well, many of us do what we do when we feel physical pain—whatever it takes to make the pain go away. Often, that means figuring out how to fit in with someone else's idea of "normal." Coping mechanisms can include mimicking[6]—changing the way we dress, speak, or otherwise comport ourselves to match the people we want to accept us (while reverting to our most authentic selves when we're back in our comfort zones, a strategy called code-switching)—or complying[7] with their demands in the hope of gaining their favor. For BIPOC, it can mean hewing as close to white ideals of beauty as possible, such as stripping down your fashion and makeup preferences, straightening your hair, or for men, shaving a beard even if it's worn for religious reasons. For people who identify as LGBTQ+, it might mean wearing gender-conforming clothes (clothing that corresponds with the sex you were assigned at birth), or letting people assume your partner is of the opposite sex, or pretending a same-sex partner is just a friend or roommate. Many times, in our desire to be perceived as "normal," we exclude ourselves to ensure inclusion. We hide and pretend. We smile all the goddamn time to make sure we don't look "angry" or "scary." We avoid bringing up certain topics, and when we can't, we keep our opinions neutral. We adhere to expectations that we can't and don't want to live up to. We stay silent when we know we should speak. We get the costume just right, make sure it doesn't slip, and with a little luck, we're allowed to belong and even rise.

Within organizational settings, Dr. Patricia Faison Hewlin refers to these coping mechanisms as "façades of conformity," and her research shows that BIPOC, and Black people most of all, feel especially pressured to hide behind them.[8] For some people, it works. The pain goes away. Yet while conforming to "normal" may be protective, it can also be a form of bondage. I don't know this to be true because I read about it in a scientific journal. I lived it.

HIDING IN PLAIN SIGHT

I spent years on the struggle bus, first trying to convince business owners and company leaders to prioritize diversity and inclusion because it was the right and moral thing to do, then, when that didn't work, trying to get them to let me prove that I could open markets and create competitive advantages through diversity communication initiatives if they'd just give me a chance. I did it while hiding who I was as much as I could, and a constant trickle of reminders and warnings was ever present in my brain: *Don't sound too Black. Don't frown or be too serious so they don't think you're "angry." Careful about what you wear so they'll know you're professional. Wear your hair a certain way so they don't think you look too "ethnic."* I had a carefully designed costume, and I wore it well, even as the pressure and strain of constantly checking to make sure it was in place ground me into dust. Meanwhile, time and time again, my best "white" voice landed me in-person meetings, which were canceled or dramatically shortened as soon as my Black body made it into the lobby. *So sorry, Mr. Jones had to run out for an emergency. Apologies, it turns out I can only spare 10 minutes. Please forgive me, something has come up. Why don't you just leave me your information and I'll give you a call once I've looked it over?* They didn't want to hear what I had to say; my skin color, combined with my age (I was only 22) and gender, told them everything they thought they needed to know. Maybe it had nothing to do with any of those things, but I had nothing else to go on. If you have never had to think about your race, gender, or age playing a part in how someone reacts to you, that is privilege.

I limped along, my main source of income stemming from my side hustles, like freelance writing for local publications and teaching as an adjunct professor at our local community college. I also worked on the occasional PR and marketing campaigns focused on diverse markets or companies hit with discrimination lawsuits. Oh yes, they were quick to call when their ass was on the line, and as the sole diversity and inclusion firm in the state, I was their only hope. But getting companies to see the benefits of proactively making employees that looked like me feel welcome and included? Few saw the need, either ignoring their massive and disruptive turnover issues, or refusing to make a connection between their revolving doors and the discrimination, pay inequities, and lack of career advancement opportunities faced by their female and BIPOC employees (unprotected by the Civil Rights Act until 2020, most LGBTQ+ folks knew better than to come out at work in deep-red Oklahoma). Meanwhile, I was a member of multiple professional networking groups, including every group representing people of color, and I knew for a fact that their employees who fell into these categories were deeply unhappy and unengaged, and constantly looking to bounce.

For the clients that did commission my services, I did everything I could to downplay my real self so that once they got past my skin color we could connect, and they'd be more willing to let my ideas take center stage. I wore presentable hairstyles and business suits, and I carefully monitored my speech, praying I wouldn't slip into the natural mix of Ebonics and country that my mother and I had both tried to drum out with voice and diction classes.

In addition, if I couldn't avoid discussing my personal life, I referred to my partner, whom I'd been with for a decade, with a male pronoun, a lesson I'd learned well from an early mentor, a gay man who kept his sexuality secret for fear of losing his job. I kept it on the DL outside the office too. Since I'd been young, the message I'd heard from the pulpit, where my grandfather had preached his sermons every week until he died, was that homosexuality was sinful. I'd already seen the family freak out when a favorite older cousin came out, so when I realized I was having feelings for women as well as men, I kept it to myself. When I married a preacher at the age of 24, it was for love, but subconsciously it may have also been an act of self-preservation. There were a lot of pressures on that young marriage, but the straw that broke its back was when my husband started pastoring in my hometown. Suddenly the church ladies were calling me Sister Montgomery (my homegirls loved that), and I was getting the side-eye for skipping 3 P.M. Sunday services. I was not made to be a preacher's wife, and the marriage only lasted one year. This caused a lot of drama within the church and my extended family, and I didn't want to go through more. I'd already lost some friends who knew about my sexuality, and while I didn't think my family would disown me, I dreaded their disappointment and embarrassment.

As time went on, though, hiding who I was, at work or at home, became increasingly exhausting and enraging, especially because it didn't make a difference. No matter how much supportive data I showed them, most of corporate Oklahoma didn't see why inclusivity, welcoming people with differences, or reaching out to new markets that didn't look like them was worth their time or effort. And when I was hired, I was often grossly underpaid. The church said people like me were destined for hell, but by 2016, with most of the business community still denying it needed to change the way it recruited or treated its BIPOC employees, and crumbling under the pressure of lying about the woman I loved, I realized that I was already there. Oklahoma broke my heart. I didn't need nearly two decades' worth of social science research to tell me that ostracization registers as physical pain.

This part of my story isn't unique. There are millions of people currently feeling just like I did, some of them probably sitting just a few feet away or staring back at you on Zoom. Now, I know rejection, ostracism, and judgment are part of the human experience. Everyone has felt the sting of not getting picked for a sports team, or play, or even a school or job. Everyone's had to deal with bullies and cliques, or had their heart stomped on by someone they loved. But only some people spend their whole lives trying to keep a façade in place, so their natural behavior, appearance, or speech doesn't come across as too different, too loud, too quiet, too aggressive, or just too not-white, straight, and "normal." When people experiencing long-term ostracism figure out that no matter what they do they'll still always be "the quiet Asian guy," or "the funny fat chick," or "the lesbian,"—that they'll always be something "other," and definitely not normal—they'll often stop coping (i.e., mimicking or complying) and become resigned. Resignation can prompt aggression or apathy, as well as mental health consequences like feelings of alienation, depression, helplessness, and unworthiness.[9] It's brutally hard on our hearts and psyche to realize that our very being will always set us apart unless we commit to a lifetime of contorting ourselves into whatever shape makes straight, thin white people comfortable.

BS BREAKS US

While we're here, can we admit that these antiquated standards don't always work for a lot of white folks, either? Many white women spend an inordinate amount of mental and physical energy—energy they could be spending on thinking up innovative ideas at work—trying to shrink their bodies to fit a certain thin, willowy ideal. Heightism can affect short men's lifetime earnings in some fields.[10] And since the 1980s, the tendency for businesses to use an undergraduate degree as the end-all, be-all sign of potential leadership and competence has excluded millions of people from the kind of jobs that lead to professional advancement and the higher standards of living of the middle class. At one company where I conducted random interviews, I met a woman, Joyce, who had been successfully covering the work of the job above hers for months and thought she was a shoo-in for a promotion, until she found out the company wouldn't give her the position because she didn't have a college degree. Instead, they hired a young woman who had graduated from college a month before. Then the company asked Joyce to train this young woman for the job Joyce supposedly couldn't do. Joyce admitted that her resentment about the situation had made it impossible for her to welcome her new young boss warmly, or to offer anything but the bare minimum amount of attention the woman needed to get up to speed. Everyone on the team was pissed about what had happened, and consequently the new boss was having a hard time earning their trust and respect. Meanwhile, Joyce, feeling rejected and unappreciated, was going through the motions at work and looking for a new job. Can you blame her? After I explained what their fealty to a college degree was costing them in terms of intellectual capital from an experienced employee, and productivity from their new one, company leadership changed the language in their job postings to reflect they'd be open to considering someone who had substantial life or job experience in lieu of a four-year degree. But the damage was done. Joyce would never feel like a valuable member of the company, and she left soon after I met her.

You may not know what it's like to try to navigate spaces where you're the only person who looks or sounds like you, but I'll bet you've had to pretend to be someone you're not, at least every now and then, to get wherever you are today. Here's where the self-examination from Chapters 1–3 is about to be really helpful.

RADICAL ACT

Think back and identify the times when you might have changed or hidden your authentic self to reflect the "normal" your biasphere established for you. The classic example is the teenager who changed their clothes and hairstyle as soon as they left the house and their parents' watchful eyes. But what about as an adult? Maybe you've never admitted to your book club that you actually love romance novels, or to your fellow congregants that you've got some serious doubts about the tenets of your faith. Maybe there have been times when you've had to alter your tone or think carefully about your words to earn someone's respect. Or maybe you see a lot of yourself in the old Risha, who put on a costume and mask every day before going to work. What parts of yourself have you abandoned or hidden for the sake of others?

Next, list all the "normal" standards you've established for yourself. For example, perfection used to be my normal. When bidding for contracts, my competitors' proposals were sometimes only one page long, containing only a jargon-filled mission statement and some perfunctory information about their cost and timeline. Sometimes I found typos. Mine, on the other hand, were beautifully designed, meticulously proofread, and sometimes up to 15 pages long, outlining my credentials, services, and differentiators in ridiculous detail. (These insanely high standards aren't unusual for BIPOC professionals, by the way, especially Black women; for many of us, "Work twice as hard to get half as far" is our mantra.) Consider how you've projected those standards of normal onto others and how you've treated those who couldn't or wouldn't live up to them.

Finally, replace the word *normal* with the word *professional*. Have you made any sacrifices to fit in where you work, like shortening your ethnic-sounding name or lying about your interests and hobbies? Did you stop wearing your preferred dramatic makeup, or start wearing makeup even though you don't like the stuff? If you're a man who likes to wear nail polish, do you take it off before the end of the weekend? Without their BS in place to blind them, it's often surprising to people who conduct this self-examination to realize how often they've been willing to hide who they were or agree to things they didn't want to just to get ahead, fit in, or gain respect.

How have you judged others who didn't do the same, or who despite their efforts haven't lived up to your standards? How much has that judgment affected your perception of the quality of their work? Have you ever gone easier on someone you found attractive than on someone you found unattractive? Have you ever automatically shrugged off an applicant for a position because while they had the required undergraduate degree, it wasn't from the "right" kind of school, or assumed someone without your educational pedigree wouldn't be able to keep up in a conversation with you and your friends?

There was a time when I wanted to make sure that my employees and I exemplified professionalism. As the owner of a Black-owned business with several Black employees, I didn't ever want a client or partner to walk through the doors and find anything that could be deemed as stereotypical, i.e., their BS. So, you can imagine my dilemma the day one of my employees showed up to work with a hairstyle that I didn't consider professional. Should I send her home? I was torn. I talked to a few trusted staff members. My white colleague didn't understand what bothered me so much—she thought the woman looked fine—but my Black colleague understood.

I honestly couldn't say for sure whether I was judging this woman against my own criteria or if I was still looking at her through the lens of white society to find her coming up short. Regardless, it was a test. How long had I been saying that we shouldn't judge people by the superficialities of how they look or talk? Would I judge this woman strictly on the quality of her work, or would I cave to my insecurities and demand that she go home and not come back until she had a hairstyle that conformed to my standards of dignity and professionalism? In the end, I said nothing, and the following day, she showed up with a finished new 'do. What is important to note is that her hairstyle did not affect her job at all. She was a solid employee who did quality work. Since then, I've done more work to stretch and grow so that I can be courageous enough to allow people to be who they are without worrying about how their authenticity will affect my business, as well as courageous enough to have honest conversations with my employees when there's an issue to be resolved. This is the kind of progress and perspective shift Radical Acceptance makes possible. Without it, I would have stayed locked into my BS ideas of what was "normal" and likely taken steps that would have cost me a great employee.

It's unlikely that you've never let your BS affect the way you judge and treat people at work. My team has asked over 50,000 people who've gone through the process of examining their BS to describe their behavior around people against whom they held conscious and unconscious biases about race, sex, sexual preference, physical appearance, and yes, even professionalism. The list includes:

- Selectively avoiding people
- Selectively refusing to make eye contact or smile
- Not interviewing or hiring diverse people

- Ignoring certain people in meetings while listening to others
- Refusing to make introductions
- Engaging in favoritism
- Gossiping about people
- Questioning people's qualifications or experience
- Diminishing people's educational accomplishments and degrees by attributing them to luck, quotas, or anything other than their hard work

These are all forms of ostracism. How many feel familiar?

If you're being honest with yourself, you will probably be as surprised as most of the people to whom we posed this question to discover how many times you've pulled this crap, even if unintentionally. It's often a revelation to learn that you're not as self-aware as you thought you were. In sum, what you discover through this exercise can improve the way you treat others, and the way you treat yourself. No one, including you, should have to diminish themselves to make other people comfortable, or to convince others they are worthy of respect, attention, and advancement.

Our BS about what's normal, professional, and desirable not only denies millions of people a full and healthy work life, but it also causes countless organizations to lose out on massive amounts of human potential and talent. The system truly is broken, and everyone pays the price.

GOTTA BE ME

Right around the time I learned that my mother had a serious heart issue, an investor pulled out of my business and sent me into a financial free fall that forced me to lay off employees and close my physical doors. Teetering on the verge of a mental breakdown, I made a pact with myself. I had done everything "their" way. I'd been the establishment's poster child for "normal," for how a Black woman should look and conduct herself in order to be accepted and heard, yet they still hadn't listened. I had tried looking better, sounding better, knowing more, and demanding perfection from myself—everything my parents, grandparents, all the members of my village, and the rest of my biasphere had taught me was the secret to success in this country—and it hadn't worked. So fuck it. I was going to rebuild, and I was going to do it using my diversity as my superpower. So what if I failed? I'd already lost everything while pretending to be someone else; it couldn't possibly feel any worse doing it as my full self. As Sammy Davis Jr. sang, "I gotta be me." It was time for me to live, not merely survive.

I've never been as terrified as the day I made that decision—and never felt such peace. I challenged everything I believed and discovered that when I let go of all the biases fed to me by my biasphere, I could breathe. It freed me to appreciate all my beauty and strength, and to see the same in others. It gave me permission to stop conforming to a system that was never built for someone like me anyway. I lived and loved out loud. I publicly showed affection for my partner. I spoke freely about our relationship. I had the word *Free* tattooed on the back of my neck. My family didn't disown me, so I'd completely misinterpreted my biasphere when it came to that. They prayed a lot for me—they're probably still praying for me—but I am loved and welcomed by everyone that matters. When it came to me, they redefined their normal.

I owned everything about me, finished my first book, and started launching posts about it on social media. Shortly after, I got a call from a Kansas City bank asking if I'd come speak to them about unconscious bias. After that event, a bank in Chicago got in touch about an event. I asked if they'd been recommended to me by the bank in Kansas City. They hadn't. They'd just read my posts and LinkedIn content and liked what I had to say. Then I heard from a high school in Tulsa. Each time I delivered the same message I always had, but now I also talked about my own experiences with intolerance and feeling unwelcome. And when people dealt with me, they dealt with me, not a façade of who I believed they thought I should be. Instead of scaring clients away, it brought them to me in droves. The response was overwhelming. The number of people who came up to me after my speaking engagements to warn me that I needed to be saved by Jesus were overrun by the number of people who told me I'd changed their lives and wanted to learn more. My complete and total confidence, pride, and love for who I was broke down the assumptions, mistrust, skepticism, and biases people carried into their interactions with me (often completely unconsciously). Today my company is global and I have spoken in front of audiences around the world.

With zero fucks left to give, I offered Radical Acceptance to myself and to others, no longer seeing people as a threat or fearing they'd respond to me negatively. Instead, I dealt with them as individuals. Now that I could be me, I was determined that anyone in my presence would get to be themselves too. It might be the only 30 minutes of their day in which they'd get to breathe freely, but it was completely within my power to give them that gift. It paid off too. I grew in ways I'd been working toward my entire life, and so did my business. In just three short years, I went from closing my physical doors to building a company that consistently earns seven figures a year. I wish Grandma could see me now. I did become a teacher, just as she'd hoped, with the country as my classroom. I'd be remiss if I didn't acknowledge the many companies and people in Oklahoma that believed in and supported me. Without them, I would not have made it to where I am today. They are why I can go before an audience of thousands of people staring (or, even sometimes glaring) at me and disarm them immediately.

THERE'S AN US IN INCLUSION

What if your company—whether you own it, lead it, or work for it—could offer the peace of mind of being fully seen and accepted to everyone who's a part of it? Imagine the productivity boost. The retention. The lowered health costs. The heightened morale and camaraderie. There would literally be no downside, except maybe for the few people upset to learn that they no longer got to dictate or model the standards for "normal" and "professional." I promise that not one of the companies who've adopted Radical Acceptance has ever had someone show up to work in pajamas and slippers. Radical Acceptance is not about letting people run roughshod over your dress code; it's about allowing previously marginalized people to show up to work without feeling pressured to make sure their costume doesn't ever slip, confident that they will be as welcomed, included, respected, and given access to the same opportunity and resources, as anyone who's always lived comfortably within white, straight society's rigid parameters of "normal." Is that really so hard?

I won't lie: it will be for some people. I recently spoke with two board members who'd been with a company for several decades. All remembered stories of women being chased around desks, and an especially egregious incident in which a male employee flipped a woman's skirt over her head as she walked by. At the time, these board members caught grief for mandating sexual harassment training, though it's surely clear to everyone reading why it was necessary. Today the board members are hearing similar resistance to DEI training, yet there are zero chances that it's not just as necessary as the sexual harassment training proved to be. One of the biggest disappointments in my career occurred when two reps for an Oklahoma-based client that I thought was making real progress with brought me in for a meeting to discuss some changes they were going to make based on feedback they'd received about my training. I already knew that very religious people sometimes objected to my occasional curse words, but those were bleeped out from the videos the employees watched. I also knew that a few people believed I was calling them racists. Of course, I never said anything close to that, but it's a common knee-jerk reaction from people who don't want to believe they have biases and certainly don't want to check to make sure they're not wrong. So, what was issue that precipitated this meeting? Negative feedback from the company's Black employees.

I was devastated. When I speak, train, or consult, I put my whole self into it. I work hard to deliver a message in a way that it can be received. I know I discuss things that are tough to hear and that someone will always be unhappy with me, but I am a voice for the voiceless. To learn that some of the people that I was working to make life better for were unhappy with my training felt like being kicked in the chest.

Two thoughts immediately came to mind. First, the Black community is not monolithic. Everyone doesn't have to like what I say or agree with it simply because they're Black. Second, how many people felt this way? I had to find out. I wasn't going to get any more answers out of the client representatives, so I turned to someone at the company I'd gotten to know through their DEI taskforce. This employee can only be characterized as everyone's favorite auntie and had been working at the company forever, so I knew she would tell me the truth even if it hurt.

That conversation didn't go the way I thought it would. She asked me to explain what had happened, and when I told her that the company wanted to cease the training because Black employees had a problem with it, she stopped me cold. "That's a flat-out lie, Risha." It turned out that the issue came up because nonmanagement employees wanted to know why the managers weren't being forced to take a training that the company had announced was mandatory. Only 30 percent of the managers had completed the training, and when my contact had tried to talk to some of the holdouts, they swore they wouldn't do it. One told her all he needed to do to know how to treat people right was read the Bible. What did the company do in response? They put out a poorly worded survey that asked a few questions about my training but was mostly a rehash of a nationally recognized survey they put out every year. With great trepidation, I eventually read some of the answers.

There were the expected opinions that I was racist. But one person said I hated white people. Another objected to my "homosexual agenda." One woman wrote that the minute I announced that I was bisexual, she hit the mute button so she didn't have to listen to me anymore. Someone expressed irritation with my dangling earrings, which they found distracting.

These people didn't have a problem with my training. They never even listened to what I had to say. They had a problem with me. As for the Black people who supposedly had negative feedback, there was only one, and that was a religious employee objecting to my language.

Instead of standing firm against the pushback (which they should have expected) or talking to me about the problem and looking for a solution to the problem, the company decided to withhold the training until they could agree on how to proceed. They knew they had a problem and had called me in to tell them how to fix it, then caved to the people who didn't want to upset the status quo. Worse, instead of owning their cowardice, they made the Black employees their scapegoat. I respected so many of the company's leaders so it was tough to witness how one person's opinions could undo the progress we made.

It can sometimes require deep, uncomfortable work to make sure that we're treating everyone around us with respect. As long as we keep our biaspheres firmly in place, our sense of "normalcy" can't evolve and progress. Not everyone is brave enough to do that on their own, so sometimes people in power are going to have to insist. No one's asking anyone to be perfect—everyone makes gaffes and mistakes—and no one can police people's thoughts. But we must have the courage to face our failings and commit to doing better, and when we're able, demand that others do too.

Embracing Radical Acceptance will make this work easier. It upends our definition of normal. Actually, it rejects the premise that such a thing even exists. And when we abandon that idea, there's nothing left for our biases to cling to. Ageism, classism, sexism, transphobia, you name it, without the concept of "normal" to give them oxygen, they dry up like dust. That's how embracing Radical Acceptance sets us—and everyone with whom we interact—free. That's how it makes us whole.

Making sure everyone in a work environment feels accepted, included, and valued isn't just the moral and ethical thing to do. From a business standpoint, it's a necessity. Luckily, it's not as hard as it sounds, because guess what? Just as ostracism and exclusion jolts similar neural circuits as physical pain, being welcomed and accepted—what social scientists would call social rewards—causes the brain to respond the same way as it does when we receive tangible rewards, including money.[11] The science suggests that "bringing out the best in people in the workplace depends at least as much on optimizing a person's social and emotional well-being as it does on [cognitive processes such as language, memory, and reasoning]."[12] In other words, normalizing inclusion, compassion, and equity is as important to recruiting and keeping the best employees, and creating convivial, energized work environments, as competitive paychecks and generous benefits.

FUCK FEAR, LIVE LOVE

All right, then. Once we've taken the radical act of thoroughly analyzing our unconscious BS and examining how it colors our perceptions, causes us to judge people, and compels us to sustain and contribute to an unhealthy, unwelcoming, even threatening environment for our BIPOC and LGBTQ+ colleagues, what are we left with?

Love.

Hold up. I'm not going to tell you I expect you to learn to love everybody. I know this is the part where a lot of motivational speakers will start talking about how much they love you, but that's not going to happen here. God gets to love everyone unconditionally; I don't even know you. What I do know is that the one thing we all have in common, no matter our faith or lack thereof, class, creed, color, sex, gender, height, weight, or whatever . . . is heart. We don't need to love everybody, but if we're not treating people the way they want to be treated, the way they're begging to be treated, we are not even being kind or decent. Radical Acceptance draws us a new baseline, a new normal. When we're better than our BS we break down our fear, which allows us to approach people with an open spirit and mind. That makes it possible to accept people as they are, and that, friends, is an inherently kind, decent, and yes, loving act.

If you've engaged with Part I of this book honestly, you may now be acutely, maybe even uncomfortably, aware of your BS and biased behaviors. That's what's up! This perspective shift means you're now ready for Part II, which will outline the actions you can take to reverse those harmful behaviors at work, as well as counteract any biases, prejudices, or discriminatory actions you witness there, all while granting yourself and others grace. What follows are clear instructions that won't just show you how to avoid being exclusive, but how to be intentionally inclusive and engaged.

PART II

BUILD A BS–FREE CULTURE

(RADICALLY ACCEPT OTHERS)

CHAPTER 5

JUMP-STARTING THE NEW CULTURE

Not long ago, the head of an HR department hired us to conduct a DEI baseline assessment. We scheduled five workshops for their company. They told us to expect at least 100 attendees for each.

On our best day, six people showed up.

What happened?

I knew we were in for problems during our first Zoom call with our new client. In attendance was the HR head, a VP, and the company CEO. Businesses everywhere were being pressured to reevaluate and upgrade their efforts to introduce and maintain diversity, and to address persistent complaints from their workers of color and other underrepresented employee groups. Our main contact and the VP both expressed enthusiasm for their mission and were eager to hear our ideas. The CEO, however, remained silent. Worse, his body language and facial expressions practically screamed, "I'm here because I have to be." I guessed they believed their subordinates were jumping on a politically correct trend, but that it would cause a PR stink if it got out that they'd blocked efforts to bring better DEI into the organization. They would go through the motions, but they wouldn't pretend to be happy about it.

The head of HR had told me that it was the Black employees who were most negatively affected by the culture of the company, so I thought it best to meet with them privately (and virtually, as we were still in the middle of a pandemic) so they could share their experiences and voice concerns without having to worry about how their white co-workers or bosses might react. A Black woman who couldn't make the meeting asked for a separate chat. It turned out that she had already tried bringing Black employee concerns to the attention of people in power but had met a brick wall. She encouraged me not to get my hopes up for a productive meeting; the Black employees wouldn't talk much because they knew nothing they said or that I did would make a difference. She was happy to see me there but was pretty sure I'd been called in to protect the company from being dragged on Twitter, not to implement real change. They were just following a trend.

The meeting went just as she predicted. The company didn't recruit from a diverse pool, so there weren't many POC at the company. The majority of POC they did hire worked in low-level customer service jobs and felt they didn't have a voice. Complaints about how they were expected to respond to disrespectful and even abusive customers were generally met with indifference. The only surprise was one extremely agitated employee, vocal to the point he monopolized the meeting. He'd found out that someone working the same job as he earned $15,000 more, and he was enraged.

I then hosted another conversation with a larger pool of employees that included department heads, VPs, and the CEO. During this call, the angry employee raised the issue of pay disparity three separate times. Several white female employees expressed dissatisfaction with the number of women holding leadership roles. The VP jumped in to provide a list of changes the company was making to help women feel mentored and supported so there would be more women in the pipeline when leadership opportunities arose. The CEO, however, stayed quiet through the whole meeting. Normally, when CEOs are present in meetings like this, they at least pretend to be interested in addressing employee concerns or pay the issue lip service. But not this one, and you better believe everyone in attendance noticed.

My HR contact pushed for our subsequent presentations to be mandatory for all employees, but in the end, the best we were able to get were "lunch and learns." In normal times, these would be voluntary events where the company provided a catered lunch while the attendees participated in our workshop. In the time of COVID lockdowns, there wasn't even the lure of free lunch to compel people to show up. Attendees would be sitting at home eating whatever they'd pulled from their pantries and refrigerators. I told my contact I suspected these voluntary sessions would be a waste of time. I was assured that if we factored in plenty of time to build awareness and tossed in some good marketing, people would come. But they didn't.

The lack of a mandate meant we couldn't collect the data we needed to gauge how employees felt about their workplace. Normally, after the first large meetings, we'll randomly choose some people to come in for 30-minute in-depth interviews, or IDIs. We also conduct a company-wide survey, which most companies make mandatory. When they don't, we make it our goal to get at least half the company to submit answers. This company, unfortunately, just wasn't interested. We made several marketing pushes and even extended the deadlines for people to deliver their answers, but to no avail. After we turned in what data we were able to collect from our initial assessment, we never heard from the head of HR or the company VP again.

You might think I resented the CEO for his attitude and blamed him for our inability to make any headway. I'd known as soon as I met him that the odds were against us, and obviously I was disappointed to be proven right. I did, however, appreciate that he didn't fake any interest in our project. I have some respect for that. More important, I appreciated him letting his employees see so clearly how he felt. Now they knew not to waste their time hoping things might change for the better. If DEI was that important to them, now they knew without a doubt that they needed to look for a job elsewhere.

TOP-DOWN LEADERSHIP FOR BOTTOM-UP RESULTS

Have you ever been in a relationship where you were doing all the work to keep it alive? It didn't last, did it? That kind never does. Successful DEI is no different. Like a personal relationship, it requires commitment and partnership to succeed. Just as one person in a couple can't do all the emotional heavy lifting, a company culture can't change without buy-in from everyone involved. That's not to say if you're in an entry-level position that you can't take individual steps to create change within your own sphere.

You can, you should, and every chapter in the rest of this book will show you how so you can be better than your BS. However, the most successful, culturally transformative companies fill their top ranks with individuals fiercely committed not just to the company's financial success, but to its mission. Think Zappos, Costco, or Patagonia. For a company to have far-reaching, long-lasting impact, leaders have to demonstrate their commitment in ways that inspire everyone to take responsibility for carrying out that mission. The rest of this chapter will outline the first steps every leader can take to show their stakeholders and the world they mean business. For everyone else, it shows you what to look for when job hunting or judging whether your current place of employment is serious about improving inclusivity or making superficial gestures.

Step 1

The first step to fixing any problem is to gauge how deeply it runs. To that end, I developed a DEI diagnosis to help leaders get anonymous and honest feedback about how well employees understand the concept of DEI, how much they think the company prioritizes it, and how effectively the company encourages it. We issue a mandatory survey for all employees while simultaneously conducting IDIs, asking questions such as, do employees believe discriminatory issues exist that create a toxic work environment? Taken together, the answers paint a complete portrait and set a baseline assessment of the DEI health of any company. Below are some of the questions included in our survey. If you're not yet in a leadership position, you can start taking your own company's temperature right now by answering these survey questions for yourself.

DEI SURVEY

Are you confident that you understand the meaning of diversity?*

☐ Yes

☐ No

I can voice a contrary opinion without fear of negative consequences.*

☐ Strongly Disagree

☐ Disagree

☐ Neutral

☐ Agree

☐ Strongly Agree

Do you struggle to understand the relevance of any of the following DEI issues?*

☐ Racism (prejudice, discrimination, or antagonism directed against a person or people on the basis of their membership in a particular racial or ethnic group, typically one that is a minority or marginalized)

☐ Ageism (prejudice or discrimination on the grounds of a person's age)

☐ Ableism (discrimination in favor persons WITHOUT physical or intellectual disabilities)

☐ Sexism (prejudice, stereotyping, or discrimination on the basis of gender)

☐ Homophobia (dislike of or prejudice against LGBQIA+)

☐ Xenophobia (dislike of or prejudice against people from other countries)

☐ Transphobia (dislike of or prejudice against transsexual or transgender people)

☐ Religious Intolerance (intolerance of another's religious beliefs or practices or lack thereof)

☐ I don't struggle with any of these.

What barriers prevent you from contributing to an inclusive organization?*

☐ Communication

☐ Time

☐ Resources

☐ Knowledge Gaps

☐ Authority

☐ Other:

Leadership at my company reflects the diversity of its employees and members.*

☐ Strongly Disagree

☐ Disagree

☐ Neutral

☐ Agree

☐ Strongly Agree

Your company values the differences (gender, race/ethnicity, age, sexual orientation, persons with disabilities, or veterans) in their employees and members.*

☐　Strongly Disagree

☐　Disagree

☐　Neutral

☐　Agree

☐　Strongly Agree

How does DEI give your company a competitive advantage?

_____

_____

What is one idea that could be implemented to improve DEI at my company?

_____

_____

Can you please describe the discrimination that you or others have experienced?

_____

_____

Your company encourages an environment of openness, acceptance, and the free exchange of ideas.*

☐ Strongly Disagree

☐ Disagree

☐ Neutral

☐ Agree

☐ Strongly Agree

Some of these questions may seem a little basic, but they've been carefully designed to extract a lot of information from even very short answers. Several will reveal how much resistance, fear, or confusion you might face as initiatives are introduced and established. The questions that ask people to describe their personal experiences will help you get a real sense of the overall culture of the company. In many cases, the answers show that companies are a mixed bag, effectively tackling some obvious issues but perhaps simultaneously encouraging subtle forms of discrimination.

Even without directly pointing to overt examples of racism, sexism, or other forms of bigotry, however, these answers can indicate whether the company culture is open to change vs. being closed and defensive. If you find it's open to change, do your part to keep things moving forward. If you find it's closed and you're in a position of any power, start pulling your managers in and start the conversation. You have to impress upon the company that becoming more open, accepting, and inclusive is a bottom-line issue, because as long as creativity and inclusivity are stifled, productivity and morale will suffer.

In my 25-year career, the one thing that has remained consistent is the deep divide between how leadership views diversity, equity, and inclusion and how employees perceive and experience it. As you start laying the groundwork for this new culture, you'll want to avoid a common mistake that happens even in companies with the best intentions, which is to leave employees out of the conversation. Once you do that, you can't help your employees see what's in it for them. Getting their point of view is important; listening to them will be key to developing a DEI initiative that becomes organic to your business. If you find that 60 percent of the people in your company don't embrace diversity and inclusion, and 50 percent don't know that you've done anything regarding diversity and inclusion, and 1,000 people tell you they've been discriminated against, well, those numbers tell a story. If 70 percent of your workforce identifies as white and about 70 percent of the company denies the existence of bias, but 30 percent of the workforce identifies as diverse and about 30 percent of the company believes bias is a problem, that too tells a story. At one company with over 2,000 employees, the feedback revealed that few people could even agree on the definition of DEI. So to start, we came up with definitions that everyone could work with. Then, to further their education, we developed a curriculum for an online course about all things DEI, including biases, privilege, scarcity mentality, managing difficult conversations, and other topics, that they could watch and rewatch at their convenience. Once we clarified the company's goals and knew everyone was on the same page with the same basic knowledge, we were able to smoothly introduce new strategies to encourage a more welcoming, inclusive culture.

As surveys are being completed, you can randomly ask a percentage of employees if they'll agree to an IDI. (To increase the likelihood of participation and anonymity, ideally these interviews should be conducted by an outside consulting firm or a DEI officer.) I rarely meet someone who falls into a diverse category who doesn't have a lot to say and jumps at the chance to share it. And while the people who refuse the invitation tend to be white men, I've had several white, straight Christian guys come in and shock me out of my own BS by saying, "You know what? This place is fucked up and we need you. Here's what I've seen, but no one will listen. I want to help. What can I do?"

If you were chosen for an IDI, how would you answer?

SAMPLE IDI QUESTIONS

- Do you understand how diversity and inclusion give your company a competitive advantage?

- Please give us one idea that could be implemented regarding diversity and inclusion.

- What tools and resources could help you contribute to an inclusive workplace at your company? What tools and resources (education, technology, training, tool kits, resource groups, etc.) do you think would best benefit others in the company?

- If you were in charge of supporting and promoting an inclusive work group where it was your job to ensure the ideas of all the employees were considered (diversity of thought), how would you structure it? How would this be different from the current practice in your work group? (Ex: provided meeting materials for all learning styles, listened to a new idea from an employee, provided acceptable food or beverages for all eating habits and religious beliefs, etc.)

- What parts of your identity do you feel uncomfortable sharing at work?

It was thanks to an interview like this that one supervisor I met, who was positive her company was a model of diverse harmony, learned that she had a manager who was nostalgic for the days when she could count on Black people to bring her iced tea. Like, she literally cited *Gone With the Wind* as her ideal. Fortunately, while it was fucked up for her to regret the demise of a racial hierarchy, and alarming when you thought about how many POC this manager interacted with, she didn't represent common thinking or an overall cultural pattern. She was an outlier. However, the supervisor also learned through these IDIs that many overweight people at the company felt the sting of bias at work on a regular basis. Managers regularly commented on their team members' size, or implied that weight loss might improve someone's chances at getting a promotion. Like, WTF? Those issues plus others served as the catalyst for overhauling the company's culture and beginning DEI training.

You may not uncover anything this egregious, but there will be something. Most likely, you'll hear about lots of little somethings that add up to more people than you suspect feeling mistreated, unseen, and left out of the team. Sometimes the harm is caused by sheer ignorance, not malice; sometimes you discover that a playground bully has graduated to corporate bully. Regardless of why it's happening, it's happening, and people you work with aren't giving you their best because of it.

Step 2

Next, you want to aggregate the answers from the IDIs and surveys to extract the greatest insight into the DEI health of your company. How many people say discrimination against overweight people is a problem? How many regularly feel like their expertise or even their presence at the company is being questioned? How many believe they have to lie or obfuscate information about their personal lives to feel safe at work? In the end, the goal is to be able to gather enough information to be able to measure, with regard to DEI, company strengths and opportunities for improvement. You'll use this information to develop a plan that sustains the good work already being done and shores up weaker areas. Where feasible, be sure that you include your employees' suggestions and ideas. Since you're doing all this to build an inclusive culture, you want to make sure that you have buy in from the very people who work in the environment. If they don't own it, they won't support it. Without that, it will be just another initiative being shoved down their throats. Note that you must be able to clearly articulate your strategies, actions, and the specific areas on which you'll focus your training.

One more thing. It might be a good idea to copy and save some survey answers or transcribe the IDI answers (making them anonymous, of course) that best articulate the problematic nature of the discrimination or disrespect employees are experiencing. That way, when people get defensive or suggest you're the one overblowing the issue (trust me, they will), you can show them in black and white what their co-workers have to say. It can also help people who are confused about what subtle bias looks like.

Step 3

Companies that are serious about DEI announce that priority through every aspect of their business, including their external communications. Does yours? Does your marketing use inclusive language, like gender-neutral pronouns? Does your website reflect the diversity of your company and the customers it serves? Is your recruiting material and language designed to welcome any and all interested in becoming a part of the organization? What about your social media? If you were to do a broad Internet search, would you find that your public reputation as an inclusive place to work is strong, weak, or nonexistent? Every outward-facing channel should reflect the diversity and inclusion that exists within the company itself. If that public messaging and image is weak, why should prospective employees and clients believe the internal picture looks any better?

CAPTURING HEARTS AND MINDS

Once you've identified your company's weaknesses and decided how you want to address them, how do you get everyone on board? With a powerful tool that's lacking in most DEI programs, a Culture Commitment. In the past, we drafted what we called Culture Statements for our clients, but we realized that a statement wasn't enough. Most companies make statements. At issue is whether executives and employees follow through. So, like our Culture Statements, this document outlines a company's cultural goals of transparency, honesty, compassion, dialogue, and openness. The Culture Commitment, however, also serves to respectfully ensure that everyone connected to the business understands what will be expected of them in creating and sustaining a no-BS culture. This document is key to making all the work you've done so far, and will do next, stick. It formally acknowledges that everyone has a responsibility to create a more equitable workplace. It announces that anyone who chooses to work at the organization will be encouraged to be better than their BS and spells out exactly what steps leadership will take to make sure the environment is not only safe for people to come to work as they are, but also a safe place to engage in dialogue, resolve issues when necessary, and point out where improvements still need to be made.

You might be scratching your head and thinking you've seen this before, and it's called a mission statement. Not quite. Mission statements often discuss the culture and the goals that have been set to achieve success. A Culture Commitment is something stronger. It doesn't just trumpet the company's purpose and how it plans to serve its customers. A Culture Commitment publicly admits where the company has made mistakes or has been slow to address important issues like diversity, equity, and inclusion. It not only promises to do better, it also makes employees an integral part of the process. Vulnerability will be important here for both sides. It allows you to take off the masks and truly interact with each other. Brené Brown says it best: "Imperfections are not inadequacies; they are reminders that we're all in this together."

EVERY CULTURE COMMITMENT EMBRACES THE HEART OF THE COMPANY

A culture commitment explicitly states what your culture is to the people who work there and the world at large. It also dictates what is expected of both you and the company to maintain the culture.

I've heard it said that the heartbeat of any company is its people. I agree and would add, if the people are the heartbeat, then the culture is the heart itself. The heart doesn't work if it's not beating, and a culture commitment keeps the heart pumping. It is essentially an honor agreement between company employees and leaders to be better than their BS and promise to work through any issues that keep the company from being equitable and inclusive. The culture should be about total acceptance of humanity, rooting out systems of oppression and inequity while getting the damn job done. The people should respect and uphold the culture. Period! From the CEO to the most entry-level position, everyone has a responsibility to be kind, accepting, and a collaborative co-worker. Once this is clear to every employee, they understand that the culture will not tolerate toxicity, disrespect, or any isms.

Creating any Culture Commitment requires three Radical Acts:

Check Your Culture
(Reassess Your Assets)

Are We a Radically Accepting Organization? Since your employees are the greatest indication of whether your culture is BS-free, ask them. If you allow them anonymity and promise to actually act on the information they give you, they'll give it to you straight.

Ask yourself: How are we running our company? Have we made any mistakes or committed any errors? Do we have a culture of acceptance? Is leadership aware of the issues affecting our employees? How do we treat women? People of color? LGBTQ+? Do we have pay equity?

Check Your Partnership
(Recalibrate Your Alliances)

Are We Radically Accepting Others? Make sure your company is not aligning its values with unfair policies or unjust social issues that affect employees, stakeholders, or marginalized communities negatively.

Ask yourself: Are we inclusive? Do we allow our employees to show up authentically without risking our judgment? Do we have a diverse workforce that reflects the communities we serve? Do any of our policies contain exclusionary language toward a race, religion, or sexual orientation? Do we have anti-retaliation, belonging, or zero-tolerance policies?

Check in with Employees
(Radicalize Your Culture)

Are We Showing Radical Acceptance in the World? You'll know you have a radical culture when your employees love coming to work and can freely express themselves and their ideas, when the communities you serve know that your company won't stand idly by and allow mistreatment and marginalization of its citizens, and when the world knows that your company will fight against injustices in the world.

Ask yourself: How are we making an impact? Is that impact increasing the acceptance and belonging of diverse or marginalized people? Where do we spend our profits, and is it having a positive impact on humanity?

In the end, your final document, which should be prominently displayed where employees can walk by and see it daily, could read something like this:

BS-FREE CULTURE COMMITMENT

Reassess Your Assets by taking inventory of your culture.

After deep reflection of our organizational practices, we realize that we are an imperfect company composed of imperfect people but that together we can create a thriving BS-free culture. We are committed to evaluating our internal and external processes to be better than our BS by join-ing the battle against systemic racism, heteronor-mativity, xenophobia, religious intolerance, and gender discrimination. We accept ownership of the mistakes we have made, however unintention-ally, which include:

(Here you would list your company errors and how you intend to correct them.)

Recalibrate Your Alliances by checking to make sure you are not aligned with unfair practices and unjust social issues that affect others negatively.

Furthermore, we are committed to providing an equitable workplace with focused intention to hire, identify, and promote diverse colleagues. We are not looking for cultural fits. We are looking for cultural additions. This is vital for our business to remain vibrant, current, and cutting edge. We recognize that we have not always lived up to our publicly stated goals and mission.

(You would continue by naming and validating the employee experiences that have been shared with you, explain what was problematic about the way com-plaints were handled, and elaborate on how you intend to handle things differently moving forward, or what steps you plan to take to ensure these negative experi-ences won't be repeated.)

Radicalize Your Culture by making sure your employees embrace their authenticity while the communities you serve know you are partners in the fight against injustices that affect them and your employees.

We accept that it is important for our company to reflect the world we serve. That means being socially responsible and supporting humanity, while working to maintain a strong bottom line. A diverse, equitable, and inclusive culture will be intrinsic in helping us achieve that. (You should follow up with a list of organizations you plan to support and the injustices you will take a public stand against.)

Conclusion

Any person creating a toxic work environment through discrimination, microaggressions, unconscious biases, or other BS is not onboard with a diverse, equitable, and inclusive culture. We are not the company for you, because on a daily basis, we strive to Be Better Than Our BS!

We know we are not yet where we need to be, but we're committed to figuring out how to get there. Together, we will.

Of course, your company will have to adjust your Culture Commitment to your individual needs. Some issues to consider:

- The company's past issues regarding diversity, equity, and inclusion. Be up front and transparent about them.

- How your employees feel about the company's DEI efforts currently and in the past. Be sure to validate these experiences.

- Support of organizations or community efforts that are counter to the culture you want to create. Take ideas from your employees and figure out which ones align with your company values.

HOW TO AVOID PERFORMATIVE WOKENESS

If you're going in on DEI, you have to go all in. Half-assed measures and platitudes will only get you publicly shamed. That's what happened to Jeff Bezos when he suggested employees cancel their meetings so they could make time to honor Juneteenth, without acknowledging that there are zero Black members on his executive team and that the majority of his Black employees work low-paying hourly jobs in packing, shipping, and delivery.[1] It's what happened to the NFL, which produced an ad announcing a $250 million contribution to end systemic racism, featuring the names of people killed by police like Breonna Taylor and Eric Garner, without mentioning or featuring Colin Kaepernick, whom they ejected from the league because he knelt to draw attention to the problems of systemic racism and police brutality.[2] It's what happened to Nike, which faced the wrath of many of its consumers in 2018 by making Colin Kaepernick the face of its 30th anniversary "Just Do It" campaign, yet still got blasted after releasing an ad that began, "For once, don't do it . . . don't pretend there isn't a problem with racism in America." Why? Because in 2019, over 21 percent of Nike's employees were Black or African American yet fewer than 5 percent of its directors and fewer than 10 percent of its VPs identified as such.

If the NFL had wanted the country to take it seriously, it could have released a Culture Commitment like the example shown below. Ideally, it would have begun by acknowledging how badly they handled the situation with Colin Kaepernick. The NFL could have admitted that they didn't make the effort to understand the problem Kaepernick was trying to draw attention to, and therefore missed the opportunity to be on the front end of creating change. Then they could have leaned in to Radical Acceptance.

Finally, it's what happened in the summer of 2020, as protests over the murder of George Floyd spilled into the streets. Numerous well-known companies took to their social media platforms to announce their solidarity with the Black Lives Matter movement, or at least their condemnation of bias, racism, and police brutality, and were promptly called out for having a minuscule number of POC in their workforce (Microsoft), management (Amazon),[3] or, in the case of the Washington Redskins, for the obvious insensitivity of their name[4] (in 2022, they became the Commanders).

CULTURE COMMITMENT IN ACTION*

Reassess Your Assets

We Radically Accept Ourselves and Our Organization: We the NFL accept that we are constantly evolving and have more work to do when it comes to understanding the issue of systemic racism and our organization's role in perpetuating inequality. Although 70 percent of our players yet only 6.3 percent of our head coaches identify as Black,[5] and the vast majority of our executive ranks are filled by white men, we have been too slow to recognize the urgent need for our institution to examine potential better practices and to use our platform to bring attention to the issues faced by our players and their families off the field.

Recalibrate Your Alliances

We Radically Accept Others: we acknowledge that it is Colin Kaepernick's right to authentically and respectfully speak out against police brutality and racism, and that his actions are grounded in perspectives and experiences most NFL leadership has not had.

Radicalize Your Culture

We Will Bring Radical Acceptance to the World: by radicalizing our culture. The NFL will not continue to stand by as the very people who are brutalized and marginalized look like 70 percent of our players. We will fight against immoral and economic injustice by infusing $250 million to combat systemic racism. We will conduct an audit of our organizational policies and make changes that prioritize diversity, inclusivity, community action, and our players. We will continue to bring attention to and raise awareness of our efforts, successes, and failures in this regard on our websites and at games.

*This is a hypothetical example.

CHAPTER 6

HOW TO HAVE THE HARD CONVERSATIONS

I may be a DEI expert, but I'm also human, which means I've had to break down plenty of my own BS.

For many years, even after coming out, I didn't feel that I fit comfortably within the LGBTQ+ community. Most of my perception was shaped by the flamboyant images projected by the media—the rainbows, the eclectic dress, the glitter. That wasn't my style. I resented the labels too. Gay, lesbian, bi, intersex, queer . . . who could keep up? Why did they matter so much? Being Black was difficult enough. Couldn't I just be me, Risha, without having to choose a camp? As for transgender people, I found them fascinating and perplexing. How could anyone be so uncomfortable in their own body they'd be compelled to undergo painful surgery to change it? It seemed like a lot to remember a male pronoun when my eyes told me I was speaking with someone bearing what I'd always understood to be female physical traits, or vice versa. I was sure I'd make a mistake and offend someone with my discomfort and confusion.

However, instead of researching so I could understand the issues better, I came up with a different solution. And that was to avoid trans people altogether.

I was as ignorant as ignorant can be. The sad part . . . I knew better. Worse, I made my ignorance a part of my public speaking. One of the reasons my speeches are so successful is that I don't act like I have all my shit together. I've found that telling my audiences the truth about my own biases helps us to connect. In the past, I had a stock line to express my bias toward trans people: I didn't understand boys who wanted to be girls and girls who wanted to be boys. Most of the time, the line worked extremely well. Imagine, a DEI trainer acknowledging her biases, and then freely admitting that there was a time that she wasn't doing a damn thing to address them? That's funny, right? And not what my audience expected from me. People usually related, though, because that's how most of us react to our biases.

Then one day, a trans person approached me after a talk and said, "Risha, that was a great speech and it moved me to tears. But I'm trans, and when you got to that line about your bias against people like me, my anxiety ratcheted up. Even though I was willing to keep listening despite being uncomfortable, not everyone like me will be. We've gone through a lot." My words had made her feel uncomfortable and vulnerable. They weren't funny to her at all.

Normally I don't feel like I'm doing my job if people don't feel a little uncomfortable during my talks, but this was different. By this time I'd been making that speech for years. How many people had I hurt instead of helped? How could I have been so thoughtless? As someone who knew all too well what it felt like to be made to feel unwelcome, I knew I'd fucked up big time.

Here's the part where some might expect me to say I was ashamed of myself for not realizing how thoughtless I'd been for admitting to a bias, and instead of doing something about it, using it to grab people's attention during my speech. But beating myself up over the mistake wouldn't do any good to me or to the trans people I had hurt. What would do good, however, was to accept that I was carrying some ugly BS, figure out where it came from, and do my damndest to obliterate it. I didn't want to shut people down. I wanted them to feel seen and understood, not more marginalized. I also decided to make an immediate change in how I phrased this portion of my speech.

A.S.Q.: ASK STUPID QUESTIONS

We judge and fear what we don't understand. So the only way to break down my BS was to make sure I did understand. I got to work reading as many articles, books, blog posts, and more about and by members of the trans community as I could. Despite all that, I still didn't get it. I'm usually pretty empathetic, but I simply couldn't imagine how anyone could feel like they aren't supposed to be the gender they were born as. Ultimately, what finally helped was asking a trans woman I knew—let's call her Marie—if she would be willing to answer my millions of questions.

Marie and I sat on the board of a Tulsa nonprofit together, and she had attended several of my events. There were several trans members on this board, and every time it was up to me to speak, I was so scared to screw up the pronouns that I avoided speaking to anyone one on one, especially the trans people. It was always "ya'll," and "How is everyone?" On the occasions when a trans person would speak to me one on one, I'd get so nervous I'd do whatever I could to cut the conversation short. I'd noticed, however, that whenever I slipped up and called Marie by a male pronoun—she may have been dressed and made up like a woman, but her features were still strongly male—she was always gracious about it and gave me time to correct myself without casting a judgmental look like, "Again? Really?" I thought she might be a safe person to talk to.

I didn't go to her right away. First, I contacted a mutual friend and explained the self-improvement work I wanted to do and asked whether he thought Marie would be willing to speak with me. He said he knew for a fact that she was a fan, and that he thought she'd be open to the idea. So I e-mailed her and asked if we could have a conversation. I gave her an easy out, acknowledging that I was asking a big favor and that I wouldn't be upset if she turned me down. She answered, "I welcome every opportunity I can get to help others understand, and I try to get to know people's hearts. I can tell pretty quickly whether someone is hateful, and when they're just clueless." Over the course of a two-hour lunch, clueless me asked a range of stupid questions—for example, "How can someone feel like they aren't the gender they were born in?"*—and Marie graciously schooled me.

I discovered that we had lived very different lives. As a child growing up as a boy, she was drawn to her mother's dresses, makeup, and all the things little girls were usually interested in. Of course growing up in the '50s, this was unheard of. Throughout her youth, she never felt she truly belonged anywhere. She wouldn't hear the word *trans* and learn there were others like her until she was well into her adult years. By then, Marie had been living as a straight

---

*Answer: The same way other people know unquestionably that they *are* the gender they were born in. Duh, right?

married man for decades. Her marriage ended once she started acknowledging she was trans.

She had kids with her now ex-wife, two of whom weren't speaking to her at all, one of whom was still in high school and wanted to keep her hidden from their friends. I confessed I understood this younger child's feelings, and asked Marie why she couldn't have waited to transition until her teenager was out of school. She replied, "Because I've waited my entire life, Risha. Because if I'd had to wait any more, I was going to kill myself."

I was never suicidal, but I understood being willing to do whatever it took to finally be to the outside how you felt on the inside. Marie had lost her family. She'd lost her business and had to rebuild her career almost from scratch. I felt honored that she would share such difficult pieces of her story with me. Despite our different backgrounds, we had much in common. We shared some of the same concerns. We made each other laugh. And along the way, I stopped seeing her as transgender and just saw her as a person. Just a person who had been willing to do whatever it took to live freely as her authentic self. Just like me. I had forgotten the most important reason that I do the work I do, which is to celebrate the humanity in each of us.

More than anyone, I discovered, trans people are willing to lose everything to become themselves, and I can respect that all day. Radical Acceptance can come at a cost. I also realized that it didn't matter whether I understood why boys wanted to be girls and girls wanted to be boys, because regardless, I do understand humanity. I do understand the need to live your life as who you are. The "why" was irrelevant. I'd been acting like something big was being asked of me, and in the end, all it added up to was a request by the trans community to be addressed and treated with respect, dignity, and kindness. It just wouldn't be that hard. The alternative was continuing to show up in the world every day as someone who makes other people feel like shit. Because this audience member took the time to have a conversation with me and I actually listened to understand her perspective, I'd improved my ability to encourage people to reveal their best selves and allow them to reach their creative and productive zeniths at work.

No one person could ever speak for an entire population, but I'll forever be grateful for the education Marie gave me, and I pay it forward by doing my best to pass along what I learned. As for my fear of using the wrong pronoun, that dissipated the minute I realized that all I had to do was use my manners and ask, "How would you like to be addressed?" Plus admit that I made a mistake, if so warranted. In those moments where someone's identity doesn't align with what my brain sees and I accidentally use the wrong pronoun, I ask for forgiveness immediately and try my best to correct myself going forward. I've said this a million times, but it bears repeating: we have to give each other grace as we work to be better than our BS.

THE BS CHECK

At the time that eye-opening conversation occurred, people and companies weren't yet encouraging "difficult conversations." I decided a version of it should become a standard recommendation in my DEI curriculum. I call it a BS check. It's a proactive way to practice deep listening to understand where people are coming from after you've started creating a new biasphere using the suggestions listed in Chapter 2. It looks like a coffee date, but with the express goal of learning why a person believes what they do about the world, and how they were culturally formed (i.e., how they developed their sense of style, or why they love certain kinds of music).

How to Start

Inviting someone into this conversation in a way that doesn't scare them can be a bit tricky. First and foremost, it requires transparency and patience. If your company is adopting a DEI initiative, that's a perfect entry. You could say something like, "Hey, the company has taken this on, and I've decided to take it on personally as well. I'm trying to educate myself by reading and following certain social media profiles and podcasts. I still have questions, though, and I don't have a diverse group of friends to talk to. I want to be better than my BS. We've sat next to each other for a few years now, and shared photos of our kids. Could we grab a coffee and just have a conversation?" When I approached my transgender friend, I was up front, and I also added something important: an easy way to let me down. "I'm totally cool if you don't want to do this. I get it, I'm that one Black friend a lot. I realize you may not have the energy or interest in educating me, and if you say no, I won't be upset or offended."

Obviously, this conversation will go better if it doesn't come out of the blue and you've been making the effort to get to know this person at some level for as long as you've worked together. Ask them about the books you've seen on their shelves or pictures you spotted on their desk. No books or pictures? Ask how they like to spend their weekend, or a popular sporting event or concert you know they attended. Whatever you do, don't jump out the gate asking about racism, sexism, or LGBTQ+ issues. It might come off as disingenuous. Build the relationship first.

If you already have good relationships with people of a faith, background, race, or sexuality that's different from yours, you can wait for a good moment to bring up the question organically. But no matter how well you know someone, do let them know where you're coming from and why this is important to you. Regardless of your good intentions, not everyone will react well to your request, even if they like you. It's not every diverse person's job to educate people about their lives and decisions. It is exhausting work that many people don't have the energy, time, or mental head space to help you understand. They may not want the responsibility of being your teacher. They may feel tokenized. They may feel that you have plenty of resources at your disposal, and that if you're serious about educating yourself, you won't need their help. They may be tired and mistrustful, because I promise you, they've tried talking to people like you about this stuff before, but they were dismissed or ignored. They have the right to refuse. When someone doesn't want to help you, accept it without fragility or sensitivity. It's up to you not to take it personally, respect their decision, and move on.

On the other hand, you might get lucky and find someone willing to sit down with you. Or someone might tell you that they don't have the bandwidth for this kind of conversation right now, but they'll come back to you if they ever feel up to it. Let's say they do. Now what?

What to Say

Now you ask questions, including the stupid ones. For example:

- Where did you grow up? How did it shape your perception of the world or certain people?

- Did you have many POC/LGBTQ+/white people in your community? (You'd obviously adapt this question depending on who you're talking to.) If so, how were they treated?

- Were you personally friends with any POC or LGBTQ+ in your neighborhood? At school?

- Can you recommend any podcasts, books, or movies I can watch?

Don't try to get too deep during your first meeting. Keep things short, maybe 30 minutes. If it goes well and you agree to get together again, you can work up to some of your bigger, perhaps more sensitive questions.

Remember to Listen

Before you head into your BS check, test your listening skills. Check yourself the next time you're having a conversation, any conversation. Are you actually, deeply paying attention to what people are saying, or are you formulating a response before the words have even finished coming out of their mouths? Many of us are guilty of this bad habit, but it's especially insulting when we do it to someone who's trying to share their lived experience with us. If you're white and start looking for reasons why a

Black woman might have brought an act of police violence upon herself, or refuse to hear all the evidence that supports the existence of systemic racism in housing, education, law enforcement, or health care, or if you're straight and decide that LGBTQ+ discrimination can't be all that bad because you've never witnessed homophobia or transphobia, you're essentially telling people that they can't be trusted to correctly interpret what happens to them. If you believe that you, with zero lived minutes in other people's shoes or their biasphere, have a much better developed ability to discern reality, that's a surefire way to alienate people and raise barriers.

The key for the BS check to succeed is to listen without judgment. People don't get their ideas out of a vacuum, and what seems utterly irrational and hateful to us really doesn't to them. If we want to create an inclusive culture, we must hear people out. That's how we validate, which paves the way for us to act in ways that can help people see things differently.

To work on listening without judgment, try creating your own personal Culture Commitment like the one we introduced in the last chapter.

I Radically Accept Myself: I accept that I carry biases that affect my perception of the world and the people in it, and that it can show up and negatively affect the culture at my workplace. I recognize that it's my responsibility to learn if my perspectives are harming others physically, psychologically, economically, and socially, and it is my duty to be better than my BS so I can stop perpetuating that harm.

I Radically Accept Others: I accept that other people have lived through different experiences than I have, which have affected their perception of the world and the people in it, and that their perceptions feel as valid as mine. I recognize it's my responsibility to make them aware if their perspectives are harming others physically, psychologically, economically, and socially, and help them become better than their BS so they can stop perpetuating that harm.

I Will Bring Radical Acceptance to the World: I promise to recognize my unconscious bias, confront the hard questions, and listen to the answers, even if they make me uncomfortable. I recognize that it's my responsibility to learn if my perspectives are harming others physically, psychologically, economically, and socially, and it's my duty to be better than my BS that can cause others harm. I resolve to change my behavior and make different choices so that I stop judging in the moment, start creating equitable or positive change in the world, and win humanity in the end.

A REACTIVE TOOL

The BS check is a proactive way for you to gain deeper insight into how other people think and feel so you can move through the world more respectfully and inclusively. It can also be used as a reactive tool for those times you hear something insensitive, tone deaf, or ignorant come out of a co-worker's or friend's mouth. For example, I was hired to consult with a client who had invented an automotive product and wanted some marketing advice. The inventor was an older, white male. I had just brought my cousin in to begin working with me. I wanted her to attend the meeting to learn more about my business and this product. She was running a little late and called to tell me that she was coming up but thought maybe she was dressed too casually. I didn't think much of it because she knew we were meeting with a client, so I didn't think it would be a problem.

She walked in wearing short shorts, tennis shoes, and a red bandana. During this time in my career, I didn't even wear jeans to meetings, so I was astounded. I wanted to curse her out on sight because she wasn't casual, she was unprofessional.

My client looked at her and totally stopped speaking for a few seconds, which felt like minutes. I quickly came up with an excuse for my cousin to leave. As we wrapped up the meeting, my client asked if she would be working on his project. I quickly apologized for her attire and said that she had recently started working with me and I was hoping she could add some creative input. He flat out told me that he didn't want her working on his product. I asked why, and he told me that because she wore a red bandana, she must be a gang member. I laughed out loud before I could catch myself. I could tell he was irritated. I asked, "Why would you think that?"

He said, "Didn't you see the red bandana?"

I said, "Yes, but a lot of people wear bandanas. Is there another reason?"

"It's just how she looks overall," he answered.

I commented that I thought her clothes were unprofessional for a business meeting but certainly didn't count as gang-affiliated clothing. I asked, "Is there anything else that makes you uncomfortable?"

He replied, "Well, she's Black."

Incredulously (and maybe a little too loudly), I said, "So am I!"

"Yes," he answered. "But you don't dress like that."

"I might on the weekends," I informed him.

We were both visibly irritated and frustrated. He mumbled as he walked off that he would not use my company if I allowed her to work on his campaign.

After I calmed down, I called him to let him know that I wouldn't be firing my cousin and that all Black people who wear bandanas are not in gangs. I also told him that if he decided to fire my firm, that was his choice, but that he should really reassess where his images of Black people came from. He didn't fire me, but in the end, we decided to part ways.

The best question you can start with when confronting problematic language or behavior is, "Could you explain what you mean by that?" You'll find that no one can ever explain stupidity. They hem and haw around the subject until they finally admit what they said makes no sense and is offensive. I once served as a board member of a prestigious leadership organization. One day during a meeting we were discussing how to get more diverse professionals in the program when the executive director of this statewide organization stated that they would have to lower the cost associated with the program to get more diverse people to apply. I was stunned, followed quickly by being pissed off. I almost couldn't contain myself as I waited impatiently for my turn to speak. It took all my self-control to stay calm as I asked, "What did you mean when you said the price would need to be lowered to get diverse people into the program? Why do you think professional, diverse people can't afford to pay?"

You could see the ED's face turn bright red as she realized what I was getting at. She knew that the only people who would join this program were professional, educated people who made (mostly) above-average salaries. That didn't really matter because most companies pay for their employees to go through this program anyway, but even if they didn't, these people would be able to pay their own way. Entrepreneurs are the only ones that might have an issue with the cost, which has nothing to do with diversity. With her comment about lowering the price for diverse applicants, she was revealing a particularly popular bias, which is that if we focus on bringing in diverse candidates, we have to lower our expectations and accept that we won't get the best talent. In her mind, the word diverse had immediately brought to mind uneducated, unskilled, poor people of color who couldn't fill leadership positions or pay for professional development. In fact, *diverse* people have over $14 trillion dollars to spend in disposable income, the money left over after bills are paid to do things like purchase products and services, join programs, or donate to causes.

The executive director was extremely embarrassed and called me later to apologize, admitting that what she'd said was stupid. I accepted her apology and offered her grace. I know that we all have unconscious bias and that once we realize it, those who care about others and making the world better will make different choices next time. I believed that this woman wouldn't forget the lesson and would do something good with what she'd learned.

YOU'RE GOING TO FUCK UP, AND THAT'S OKAY

"I don't talk to my Black employees." *Excuse me?* I looked at the white manager in front of me with surprise. He blinked. "That's why you called me in, isn't it? Because the whole team thinks I'm racist?" It wasn't, actually. This manager's name had been pulled for an IDI completely at random. He thought he was in trouble, but I felt like I'd struck gold. There was a story here, and fortunately, the manager was more than willing, even desperate, to share it.

As he told it, during a conversation at the office with someone unfamiliar with most of the staff, he'd described a colleague as a "tall Black woman." Somehow it got back to the woman, who angrily confronted the manager and yelled at him that she should be referred to as African American. The manager apologized immediately, but the experience left him shaken. He'd always considered himself the type of person who could talk to anybody and put them at ease, but now he didn't trust his own judgment. Terrified of saying the wrong thing again, and sure he could see disgust and rage in their eyes whenever he came near, he started avoiding his Black employees altogether, only speaking to them along with the entire group, or dispatching others as his messenger when he needed to convey information to them individually. The situation had been festering for months until he was randomly chosen to talk to me. Once he figured out that I wasn't there to investigate him specifically, he decided I was his last, best hope for redemption. What should he do?

One small innocent mistake, and you're branded a racist forever. It's the scenario that every white person fears, and the possibility of it happening is one of the main things that keeps well-intentioned white people from diversifying their friend group or being bolder in their outreach to colleagues of color or different sexualities. But tell me, if you're white and you accidentally piss off another white person (as I'm sure has happened a few times in your life), do you forever avoid dealing with all the other white people around you? Of course not. First, you might try to apologize and make amends to the white person you hurt or angered, and even their friends and family if it goes that deep. But you're aware that even if they don't want to hear your apology, so long as you don't repeat that particular fuckup, there are other white people out there willing to let you start fresh and meet you at your best. You know that the white people around you are individuals that can't be lumped together into one hive-minded, monolithic group.

It was from this angle that I approached the manager. I told him that I believed the woman who was angry with him could have handled the situation much better. Though to me, the terms *African American* and *Black* are interchangeable, to this woman (and many others) they weren't, and we had to respect that. Why she lost her mind over it, I couldn't guess, but clearly a more effective solution would have been to calmly explain to her manager that in the future, she'd prefer to be referred to as African American. However, I asked the manager, "If she'd been white and stormed in demanding to be called Caucasian instead of white, would you have stopped talking to your white employees?" He thought about it for a second and replied that he wouldn't have.

"Right," I said. "So why would you stop talking to your Black employees?"

And he said, "I guess I'm more comfortable talking to white people."

Now we were on to something. The guy who thought he could "talk to anyone" had just admitted he was more comfortable talking to white people. I encouraged him to Assess his BS to figure out where his discomfort in talking to POC, however small, was coming from. Then I advised him to call this woman in for a meeting and ask if she would please explain her position, not to justify herself, but so he could be sure he understood. Once he'd gained clarity, I thought it would be a good idea to call a meeting with his entire team and explain that it had been brought to his attention that he'd made some employees feel disrespected, and that he was sorry and wanted to do better. He needed to make it clear that he was open to critique and wanted to do whatever it took to make the team become more cohesive. He could offer some ideas and solicit some from the team.

The worst thing about this story wasn't that the manager had made a mistake. We all do that. The worst thing was that instead of doing his best to solve his problem, the manager had retreated in fear. Just like pushing back on injustice or fighting for what's right, becoming better than our BS can require courage. If you admire the people who fought for human and civil rights, from abolitionists to suffragettes to Freedom Riders to Harvey Milk, remember that they did it without knowing that one day they'd be lionized for their work. In the moment, standing up and speaking out was uncomfortable and sometimes dangerous. For many people today who continue to press for a more radically accepting world, it still is. I'm not suggesting we all have to become activists—we're not all built for that. But the least we can do is be willing to step outside our comfort zone if that's what it takes to right our wrongs. Sometimes the bravest thing we can do is simply apologize.

KNOW WHEN TO HOLD AND WHEN TO FOLD

I wish I could say that after I started researching the trans world and actually getting to know a trans person, I never made anyone feel less-than again. I did, though.

I could have just taken the problematic line out of my speech altogether, but I chose not to because it was still my truth, and it did resonate with a lot of people. Instead, I changed my speech up a bit and added new material to prove that I'd evolved beyond my biases. Now when I'd come to the confession that one of my biases was that I didn't understand girls who wanted to be boys and boys who wanted to be girls, I'd pause for effect. Then I'd say, "If you're trans or you know or love someone who is, let me be clear that I realize how ignorant that statement is. But it's where I started my journey, and unfortunately, it is where a lot of you still are."

That segue led to an explanation of my self-education and how in the process I'd gotten to know trans people. Finally, I'd add, "I have to say they are some of the most courageous people I've ever had the opportunity to meet."

Some people won't give us grace and space unless we abandon our truth and come around completely to their way of thinking. One day at a talk in Pennsylvania, a woman dramatically stood up and walked out as soon as I mentioned my bias against trans people, before I could get to the next part where I admitted how dumb my bias was and the steps I'd taken to break it down. A few more people, probably friends of hers, followed a few seconds later. I noticed, but in the moment I didn't connect the words coming from my mouth to their behavior until afterward, when I was in the hallway talking to some attendees and heard the first woman speaking. I could tell from her tone she was upset, and now that I could hear her voice, I knew she was trans. That's when everything clicked. As we reentered the room, I caught up with her and asked if I could talk to her. My plan was to make sure she was okay.

If looks could kill, I'd be dead. She was pissed. Really, really pissed. "I didn't appreciate what you said," she began.

I was taken aback, but I kept a smile on my face and my tone friendly as I explained that had she listened for half a second longer, she'd have heard me admit how ignorant my bias was. "Your friends had to have heard it. I hope they told you."

That did it. Now she was in my face, screaming at me that it didn't matter what else I said; I was disrespectful. She was so angry, I started to wonder if she was going to hit me. No matter what I said to try to deescalate, she wasn't having it. She couldn't hear me. She wouldn't. I finally told her she needed to back up, and before I could lose any more of my professional demeanor, I walked away.

LEARN TO ACCEPT CRITICISM

It was the kind of confrontation we all fear, one in which good intentions are misconstrued and make us decide our efforts to reach people are pointless, and it will be safer to stop trying. But I didn't stop. I'm a DEI speaker, and I believed that common sense could tell anybody that I wasn't going to let problematic comments linger. I was gonna bring the message home. The first trans woman who critiqued my speech with her forthright but nonjudgmental approach made it possible for me to hear her criticism and think through how to fix the problem, even if I did it imperfectly the first time. My next critic wasn't as gracious, but that didn't mean her criticism wasn't warranted.

After I'd cooled down, I stopped looking for reasons why she was mistaken and focused instead on where she had a point. It didn't take long to realize that it might be difficult for someone who has been through the hell that most trans people have suffered to listen to someone you think is going to make you feel worse than you may already feel.

The last thing in the world I want to do is hurt people. Today I preface that part of my speech by warning people I'm about to make a statement that in other settings might make them consider clicking out or walking away, but that it's necessary to highlight my own weaknesses, and if they can give me a second of grace and let me share my message, they won't regret it. It seems to work, and I haven't heard any complaints since I implemented the change.

KNOW WHEN TO QUIT

Unfortunately, a BS check won't work on everyone. That's okay. In the end, if someone doesn't want to learn, and doesn't care that they're hurting others, there's nothing left to do. A final statement to make your point could be something along the lines of, "From your perspective and in your circles, that statement might be cool, but in this office it's inappropriate and hurtful." And then, depending on how much clout you carry, you can ask them not to say it anymore out of respect for their co-workers, or tell them you expect them to leave it at the door when they come to work, period.

What's important is that we learn to spend our time and energy creating change where it will be received. What's important is that even as your company works to become more inclusive, or even if your company chooses not to, you still have the power to create that inclusive culture around you whether you're in a decision-making position or not. Every effort makes a difference, and you can make this one on a daily basis.

GRACE MAKES US BETTER

We have to give each other grace. My biggest regret is that I couldn't get through to my angry critic that day in Pennsylvania, and that she'll probably always think I'm transphobic. I won't lie—it bothers me to know someone feels that way about me. It's an affront to all the work I've done in my adult life. But there's likely nothing I can do to change her opinion, and I've had to move on. Which is exactly what I'm going to ask you to do if the worst happens and one of your bias checks becomes confrontational or otherwise goes south. You have to keep showing up, because when you do, most people will see who you are. You can't worry about the few who don't. Those may be the people you need to talk to the most, but I'm giving you permission to cut the conversation short. If you can't have a rational discussion, one where you're allowed to speak and they're allowed to speak and you really listen to each other, it's wasted time. That's not going to be productive. The people who want to have that conversation, who want to help you learn or to learn more themselves, will meet you where you are. And if you can make each other laugh, even better. Laughter is one of the best ways to dissipate our differences. It doesn't mean you'll agree on everything in the end, but a respectful exchange of perspectives and ideas leaves the door open to talk to each other again someday. We can't understand each other if we can't talk to each other.

If people are so afraid of being branded for making mistakes, they'll stop trying; if people get consumed with anger, they won't be able to forgive. And then nothing will ever change. To build an inclusive, accepting world, we have to be willing to fuck up, maybe more than once. We have to be brave enough to ask the stupid questions and have the hard conversations in order to learn.

When you do screw up, if you're clear about your intentions, people who really want to encourage change will accept your apologies and move on, so long as you continue to try to do better. Others will hold a grudge and decide that no matter how much you grow or evolve, you're always going to be racist, misogynistic, or sexist. Nothing you can do about that but prove them wrong through your words and deeds. We mess up all the time because we're human, and for some of us it takes a number of knocks to learn our lesson and quit repeating our mistakes. But ultimately, if we keep trying, we get better.

EVERYONE NEEDS BIAS CHECKS

A couple of years ago, I was invited to a dinner designed to bring people together who wouldn't normally interact. Of course, I was thinking it would be no big deal since talking to people who don't see the world the way I do is what I do for a living.

That was before I sat down at my table. Seated next to me was a bald guy with a tattoo reading "666" spread clear across his forehead. As open-minded as I try to be, that tattoo made me uncomfortable. It wasn't the tattoo itself—I have three of them. And I normally don't care what people choose to do to or with their bodies. Yet this felt different. I'd broken bread with many different kinds of people, but a Satan worshiper? I tried to lean in to Radical Acceptance, telling myself this was just a man like any other, and there was no reason to be suspicious of him, but my BS was in overdrive. What if my family and millions of others were right and Satan did exist? What if this guy put a hex on me? My BS was screaming that this man had to be evil.

Then I tuned in to the conversation he was having with the person seated across from him. They were discussing PTA meetings. PTA meetings? Then he surprised me more. Even though I don't have kids, he found a way to include me in the conversation so I wouldn't feel left out. Dude had manners. And he seemed . . . normal. Like, nice. Friendly.

I kept my guard up, but now that I sensed how approachable the man was, I started to wonder, did he know there was something he could do about that tattoo? Surely he'd remove it if he could. Coincidentally, that morning I'd read a local newspaper article about a tattoo parlor that one day a year would remove gang-related or racist tattoos for free. That day was today. I went back and forth about whether to bring it up in my head:

I should tell him about the article in today's paper.

Look at him. He obviously doesn't read the paper.

Besides, it's none of your business.

But he doesn't know! I'd want someone to tell me. He's gonna be so grateful.

What the hell. I went for it. As casually as I could, with the widest, most innocent smile I could muster, I said, "Hey, I'm not sure if you saw today's paper, but I read that there's a tattoo shop removing gang-related and racist tattoos for free, today. It's not too far from here."

I tried to sound caring, but in hindsight I was projecting all my BS onto him.

He laughed. "You're the fifth person today to tell me about that article."

The woman sitting on his other side, also heavily tattooed, leaned over to tell me, "I was the first." Turned out she was his wife.

Then he schooled me. The tattoo wasn't Satanic; it was the name of a gang he used to belong to, the Rolling Sixes. He'd joined at a young age and as a result had spent the early part of his life in and out of jail. Somewhere along the way he decided to take a new path, and somehow he was allowed to quit. Yet though he changed his life completely, he left the tattoo there because he wanted to be an inspiration to other gang members who might be looking for a way out. As a result, he'd led many people to leave the gang life behind. "It's a huge price to pay," he said, "especially for my wife and kids. But right now, I feel like I owe this back to the world."

I'm sure I looked the complete fool as I tried to apologize for my ignorance and assumptions, but he was gracious and kind. I couldn't believe that I'd allowed my BS, based on nothing more than a person's appearance, to let me treat this man the same way folks have treated me and millions of others who look like me for years. I'd prejudged him and made assumptions about his character and intelligence before he'd even had a chance to introduce himself to me.

I regret to say that the experience didn't cure me. I still have biases. They don't ever go away altogether, even for someone like me who thinks about this stuff for a living. What does happen, though, if you're willing to aim for Radical Acceptance, is that when they flare up, you recognize them immediately, and that gives you a chance to make a different decision in the moment. To avoid saying the hurtful or ignorant thing. To behave with kindness instead of suspicion. To keep your mouth shut and really listen. To stay calm and stay positive when trying to get people to see your perspective instead of stooping to scorn and insults against people with whom you disagree. Each time we make a small change in the moment, we promote and encourage others to change, until eventually, to paraphrase Lin Manuel Miranda's *Hamilton*, a moment becomes a movement.

This book is primarily written for people who don't frequently find themselves in the minority at work, but the stories in this chapter highlight the fact that everyone, including diverse populations, can benefit from bias checks. Many BIPOC and other marginalized communities can be so traumatized from their experiences, they're incapable of noticing when something has shifted, or acknowledging when an individual or company is trying to change for the better. A lot of BIPOC are tired, and it's going to take more than a few smiles and signs of friendliness for anyone to prove their unbiased bona fides. Anyway, most of us can cite plenty of examples where smiles and friendliness were simply veneer overlays hiding deep layers of BS. Yet despite having experienced some really fucked-up things, it's simply not true that everyone is constantly trying to marginalize us. They're just not. Our biaspheres are as skewed as anyone else's. So while some of us may have more work to do than others, every one of us should be looking for opportunities to conduct bias checks. Because every time we actually get to know a person for who that person is, and not the group they belong to, we're all better off.

So keep talking to people and ask your stupid questions. Sometimes it won't go well. Do it anyway. You can fix your mistakes, but you can't fix anything else if you're not willing to risk making them.

CHAPTER 7

DETOXIFYING WORK ENVIRONMENTS

From Micro-Aggressions to Micro-Inclusions

There are days when I can't get anyone to say a word during a training, and then there are days on the opposite end of the spectrum where everything gets said, and shit blows up. A training at an oil and gas company was one of the latter. The crew I was addressing was tight knit. They had to be, seeing as how they spent months together out at sea on giant barges doing the specialized work of constructing pipelines and laying them on the ocean floor. Pipefitting is a heavily male-dominated field, and in the whole company of people who did this kind of physical work, only two were women. All the other women worked in the office.

I never know what to expect when I walk into a training. Will my audience be receptive? Resistant? Combative?

I was thrilled to find this group engaged and willing to participate. Everything was going smoothly until I got to the part of my talk where I introduce the concept of microaggressions. And then, fireworks.

WHAT'S A MICROAGGRESSION?

Microaggressions can be words or actions. Verbal microaggressions are small comments that take subtle digs at stigmatized or culturally marginalized groups. They frequently sound like compliments, but in reality, all they do is highlight someone's otherness, and when they're repeated frequently or accepted as part of the culture, they can be largely responsible for creating a toxic work environment. For example, telling someone her new hairstyle looks "professional," especially if it's a Black woman who went from natural to a pressed, straightened (i.e., Caucasian) style. The implication is that her hair didn't look professional before. Refusing to learn how to pronounce someone's foreign-sounding or unusual name is a microaggression. You're implying that their name is "weird" and in addition that the bearer of that name isn't important enough to put in the effort to get it right. When Mike, who we met at the beginning of this book, told me I was a credit to my race? Microaggression. He claimed all he meant was that I was cool, but what he was actually saying, even if he didn't realize it, is that most of the people of my race are some kind of bad, and that it was just amazing that somehow I came out okay.

Here's a list of some of the most common microaggressions:

- Asking "Where are you from?" or "Where were you born?" based solely on how someone looks: Implies a person is not a U.S. citizen.

- "You speak such good English!" Assumes that English is not a person's first language.

- "You're a credit to your race." Implies that the person's racial background is generally inferior or lacking.

- "You're so articulate." Implies that the person's culture is usually inarticulate.

- "When I look at you, I don't see color." Denies the person's racial/cultural identity as relevant.

- "There is only one race, the human race." Denies the person's racial/cultural identity as relevant.

- "I'm not racist. I have Black/Latino/Asian friends/family." Implies immunity from racist behavior or viewpoints because you are related to or associate with POC.

- "As a woman, I know what you go through as a racial minority." Falsely equates gender oppression with racial oppression.

- To a Black person, "Why do you have to be so animated/loud? Calm down!" Implies that differing communication styles are inferior. Tone policing, as this microaggression is called, allows the microaggressor to deflect criticism by focusing the conversation back onto how the aggrieved party is speaking rather than acknowledge and address the actual problem that needs to be discussed.

- **To an Asian or Latino person: "Why are you so quiet? We want to know what you think. Be more assertive. Speak up!"** Implies that differing communication styles are inferior.

- **"You people . . ."** Implies a negative sweeping generalization.

- **"I believe the most qualified person should get the job."** Implies that some people aren't qualified for the positions they are chosen for and are selected solely on the basis of race and culture.

- **"Everyone can succeed in this society if they work hard enough."** Implies that people of color, women, or LGTBQ+ people— the groups that traditionally face more obstacles in reaching their goals than white men—don't work hard enough and denies the existence of the systemic racism and sexism that limits these groups' opportunities for economic and social mobility.

Microaggressions can be completely accidental. During a virtual workshop for a big government client, I asked participants to send me examples of their biases. I started reading the anonymous replies aloud, and to my surprise someone said they were biased against Arabs. I've seen people admit to Islamophobia, and I've seen them write that they're suspicious of Muslims. But Arabs? That was unusual, and I was already formulating thoughts about what I wanted to say about it as I started to read the answer. Because I was distracted, when I got to the word, I started to speak, then paused before finishing the word. So instead of saying "Arab" the way it was supposed to be pronounced, it came out of my mouth as "Ay . . . Rab." And though I knew I'd jacked up the pronunciation, I compounded my mistake. Instead of acknowledging what had just happened and apologizing immediately, I moved on with my talk.

Shortly afterward, I received an e-mail from the client. There had been an Arab American in the workshop, and he'd let my contact know that the moment had made him extremely uncomfortable. Of all places, he thought a presentation with a DEI expert would be a safe space. The client was gracious and gave me the benefit of the doubt that the gaffe had only been a slip of the tongue. Still, it was important to them that I understand that my pronunciation showed a lack of sensitivity and preparation.

I was mortified by my fuckup. Not only had I lobbed a microaggression at an unsuspecting participant in my very own keynote, but also I'd set the worst example possible by failing to acknowledge it and take accountability right away. I fell all over myself apologizing to the client and asked if I could speak directly to the person I'd offended, but they told me that wasn't necessary. I was never able to get any closure, and while I hate that, I have forgiven myself because we all make mistakes and I did everything I could to rectify the situation.

Other microaggressions are silent but convey the message loud and clear that the recipients deserve suspicion, don't belong, or should be lumped together. Demanding that a Black man wearing a sweatshirt and jeans show his

ID to prove he really is a lawyer for the firm when you find him in the office on the weekend, when white people are never questioned when they show up in their casual clothes to work ungodly hours in that same building, is a microaggression. Pulling your purse closer to you on public transit or clutching it tighter when Black men walk by is a microaggression. Steering a customer toward a less expensive item in your store based solely on their race or clothing, being incapable of noting the difference among the few Asian employees at your company, or taking it for granted that a person is heterosexual—all microaggressions. They're small, subtle acts that make a person feel othered. Some of the most common microaggressions are often directed at Black women's hair. It would take a whole book to outline the long, fraught history of Black women being belittled and discriminated against for not living up to the white beauty standards that for centuries have been held up as the ideal, especially soft, usually straight hair. That history aside, have you ever thought about what an intimate act it is to run your fingers through someone's hair? We do it to our lovers, to our children, and to ourselves when we're styling ourselves in the mirror. So tell me, how in the hell does it seem okay when you're out and about to put your fingers in the hair of a perfect stranger or someone you don't know very well? I don't even want my friends touching my head. It takes me a long time to get my hair looking the way I like it. You touch it with your sticky fingers, and now I've got to find a mirror and see what damage you did. Just stop.

Seriously.

Please. Stop. Touching. Our. Hair. We do not want to be petted.

By the way, in my talks, this is usually about the time when a bald person will stand up and say, "Hey, could you tell everyone that us bald guys hate having our heads touched too?"

While I'm at it, a pregnant woman's belly isn't yours to touch either, no matter how glorious you think it is. You wouldn't touch her so intimately if she weren't carrying a baby; her pregnancy doesn't suddenly erase her right to her personal space.

Do any of these things at a company that has done any DEI work at all, and expect a call from HR. Keep your hands to yourself.

WE'RE OFTEN OBLIVIOUS TO OUR BS

Back to the pipefitters training. I'd introduced the idea of microaggressions and asked people to offer some examples. Someone wrote a comment about men (I can't remember the specifics) and I took the opportunity to talk a bit about how men could be more inclusive and supportive of women. Most of the men in the room were nodding in agreement, when a woman I'll call Marge spoke up: "What you're saying sounds great. I wish I got more of that from the men on my team." Several of those men were in our group and had just been nodding along with me. They seemed genuinely wounded to hear that a colleague thought they weren't supportive. Their surprise seemed to get her more worked up. "It happens all the time!" she said, pointing toward her colleagues. "We all use the same equipment and most of it is about pushing the right buttons; almost none of what we do relies on any kind of actual physical strength. And even if it did, I've been here as long if not longer than most of you in this room. I proved a long time ago I can do this job and that I'm good at it. Yet every day you follow behind me to check my work, testing to make sure the bolts are tight enough. I'm fucking sick of it." Man, she was pissed.

The shock on her co-workers' faces was almost comical. It was obvious they had no idea what Marge was talking about. They weren't defensive; they were just dumbfounded. Several spoke up and assured her that they checked everyone's work, but Marge was having none of it. "I've been watching for over a year. You don't check any of the men's work, even guys who just started last month. Only mine, and it's because I'm a woman." Every protest that she was mistaken or taking things too personally only made Marge angrier. For years she'd been hiding her rage to get along, and now that she had a chance to let it out, she wasn't holding back.

Eventually I had to step in and explain to the men that even if they hadn't intended to signal that Marge wasn't an equal member of the team, that's how their actions had been received. I also told them I could see they were genuinely sorry that one of their crew members was upset with them, and that even if her accusations of unconscious sexism were true, their impulse to make sure everything was done perfectly came from a deep sense of responsibility. The consequences of a poorly connected pipe or a slightly loose bolt could cause catastrophic environmental damage and even loss of life. Still, they had two choices. (1) They could try to convince Marge that she was mistaken, and that they hadn't done anything wrong, or (2) they could take a hard look at their behavior to see if they were acting on any BS that they didn't even know existed. One option would essentially tell Marge that she wasn't experiencing what she was experiencing, and likely lead to increased tension and resentment among the team in the future; the other option could not only improve the team's working relationship, but also potentially improve their other personal relationships too. It was up to the men to decide which would be the more productive path.

Unfortunately, I hadn't been brought to the site in a consulting capacity, so I couldn't walk this team through the steps of assessing their BS, but if I'd been able to, these are the questions I'd have encouraged them to ask themselves:

- Why do I check Marge's work?

- Who else's work do I check as regularly as Marge's?

- Marge had been working at the company for many years. Would they have hired her, and would she have lasted that long, at a job where shoddy workmanship or work ethic could get people killed if either of hers were questionable?

- Had Marge ever given them a reason to believe her work needed special supervision?

- Was Marge more likely to make a mistake than a man? If you believe so, why, and what evidence can you produce?

I'd then encourage them to think about the five rings of their biasphere—Family, Religion, Peers and Friends, Schools or Government, and Mass Media—and consider where any biases they discover might have come from. If they found those biases unsupported by objective evidence accumulated over the years (as is usually the case), I'd suggest it was time to redefine their "normal" assessment of women in the workplace and think about how they could incorporate Radical Acceptance and inclusion into their company culture.

This wasn't the first time I'd seen women react strongly to the topic of microaggressions. When I spoke at a Minnesota conference for engineers, a table of men fell into a conversation in which almost all agreed they were glad to have grown up with stay-at-home moms, completely oblivious to the one woman sitting in their midst, whom they knew was a working mother. They acted like she wasn't even there, yet it felt like they were talking straight to her. Whether she was working because she had to, or because she wanted to, was irrelevant. Their insensitivity made her feel like they must look down on her. She came up to me in tears and told me how they'd made her feel like shit, and all I could do was give her a hug, because there was no way to address the problem. The men had fucked up, and they didn't even know it. I often wonder how the dynamics of that team changed after that conference now that the woman knew what the men thought about moms who also had careers. There is still a lot of radical work that needs to be done to help women feel fully welcome in the workplace.

COMMON RESPONSES TO GETTING CALLED OUT

Even without knowing whether the team assessed their BS, Marge's story has a good ending. The guys listened, apologized, and promised they wouldn't do it again. Believe it or not, that's huge. The sad truth is that in many cases like these where we express that we've been hurt by something that was said or done, what we get in response is defensiveness, even outrage, that we could be offended by something so "innocuous." I understand the impulse to defend yourself. After all, you're a good person. You try to treat people well, and if you have kids, you teach them to do the same. You've never discriminated against anyone in your life, and maybe you even have a pride flag prominently displayed in your front lawn. Yet here you are, doing your best, and now someone is telling you that this totally small thing is a big deal when it's really not. It doesn't feel fair. And so you might say, "I didn't mean it that way," or "Quit being so sensitive," or if you were saying something funny, "Where's your sense of humor?" Or if you're feeling particularly exasperated, "You can't say anything anymore!"

Let me take a minute to explain why most of these answers can make members of diverse or marginalized communities feel hopeless, exhausted, and sometimes even enraged.

I Didn't Mean It That Way

When I was about 15 or 16, I was working at a local supermarket and carried some groceries out for one of our older customers. After I'd settled all the bags into the car, the lady gave me a nickel and said, "Why, you're one of the prettiest little colored gals I've ever seen." Ouch. I'll bet that woman truly believed she was paying me a compliment too, instead of revealing her racist belief that Black girl beauty was in a different and lesser league than white beauty (not to mention her resistance to dropping a Jim Crow term that considerate people had abandoned over two decades earlier). The nickel tip kind of pissed me off too.

Microaggressions can be intentional, but in most cases the perpetrator is completely unaware of the hurtful impact of their words or actions. The disparity between a microaggressor's intent and impact usually exists because they've been so steeped in this kind of language or behavior, it never occurs to them that there's anything wrong with it, and they don't have to think about it because it never affects them anyway. They're often ignorant of the history that packs the punch behind their words. My grandma Ola Mae loved garage sales, and I spent many days rising at the crack of dawn so we could get first dibs on the possible treasures we might find displayed across someone's driveway. Grandma always went in ready to negotiate. "Don't ever pay full price," she'd advise me sagely. "You've got to Jew them down." This from the kindest, most loving soul you've ever known. Had she been aware that the phrase "Jew down" was rooted in ugly anti-Semitic stereotypes depicting Jewish people as stingy, greedy cheaters, she never would have said it. I didn't hear it often, fortunately. I was an adult before I realized it was a slur.

If you're thinking it should have been obvious to me or Grandma that the term was derogatory, let me ask you, have you ever said you felt *gypped*? It comes from *gypsy*, a derogatory word for the Roma people, marking them as thieves. Have you ever warned someone not to *go native*? British colonialists used this term to caution their fellow white people not to get too comfortable with what they perceived as the inferior societies, cultures, and customs of the sprawling collection of countries they occupied. Today there's a push for us to stop describing things we don't like or consider deficient as *lame*, given that it's an insult to people with physical disabilities. Mental health advocates have started encouraging us to stop using the words *insane* and *crazy* as negative adjectives. To those who might think that's asking too much, consider what Azza Altiraifi, a researcher at the Center for American Progress, said in an interview for NPR: "It tells people like me that my life is not worth that adjustment."[1]

Our language is packed with words and idioms spawned from centuries of racism, bigotry, and ableism. It can take years for those who feel their sting to raise enough awareness around their hurtful origins or to build support for adopting more neutral or even positive substitutes. It doesn't matter how you meant your words or actions to come across. What matters is how they felt to the person who was on the receiving end.

Quit Being So Sensitive

The truth is, when looked at objectively and dispassionately, when compared to some of the horribly overt racism, sexism, or bigotry that people used to drop without batting an eyelash, your microaggression may not seem to be that big of a deal. The most painful thing about microaggressions, however, is their cumulative effect.

Almost 100 percent of the time, when I help a company confront trust or communication issues, we find that at its core the real problem is poor communication. In cases that involve microaggressions, the insult or behavior that causes an uproar or demands an intervention from management is simply the last straw, not the first offense. Many BIPOC and LGBTQ+ will tell you that every morning before they leave for work, they steel themselves against the small, subtle slights and insults they know will come at them. Each time a microaggression hits, it's like a tiny paper cut. You can't really see the damage. It stings, but not unbearably so. Certainly on its own it's not enough to derail your day. But what if it's the five hundredth paper cut? The thousandth? The ten thousandth? Put all those minuscule, invisible cuts together, and you feel like you're just one big raw, gaping wound. I hope this helps you understand why someone at the office might react to your innocent comment or question in a way that might seem over the top. You're just living through a somewhat uncomfortable blip in time. The person you just slashed with your microaggression was already nursing countless other cuts, and maybe even bleeding out. I'd almost rather someone shoot me point blank with an obvious slur than suffer unending microaggressive cuts to my self-esteem and self-confidence. When you're getting them from all sides at the office, it adds up to a toxic work environment.

It Was Just a Joke

Here's a good rule of thumb: if you make a joke at someone else's or a group of people's expense, and you're the only one who thinks it's funny, or only people who look or sound like you think it's funny, it's not funny. If you'd be uncomfortable telling that same joke in front of said racial or cultural group, it's not a joke you should tell anywhere.

There are special cases in which people who are tight with each other might be able to share dark or caustic humor that would be unacceptable in any other circumstances or in any other circle, but those tend to be few and far between. To assume anything goes anywhere is dangerous and sets people up for harm. This is how a white man—a guy known for his social justice work—got the mistaken impression that when we were introduced at a bar, where I'd gone to hear a band I liked, that it would be fine to greet me with, "What's up, N-word?" He seemed surprised when I didn't take it well. At all. I don't even let friends call me that, and he was no friend. First, he responded to me like I'd overreacted, then for the rest of the night he tried to follow me around and talk, refusing to listen when I told him to leave me alone. He finally left, but my night was ruined. To be clear, what he said wasn't a microaggression; it was flat out racist.

You Just Can't Say Anything Anymore

It might surprise you to learn that I don't want to live in a world where people feel like they can't say anything anymore. I've met a number of male clients who tell me they've stopped complimenting women when they notice they've adopted a new hairstyle or are wearing something particularly flattering. I think that's a shame. Is it really that difficult to see the difference between commenting that someone looks nice today, and commenting on their body, or between paying a compliment in a nonthreatening way and making someone feel like her space is being invaded or that you're leering? For other types of compliments, it's really very simple: a real compliment affirms something positive about someone without tearing down another person or group, or without holding up the object of your admiration as an outlier within the group they belong to. A microaggression inherently relies on drawing a negative comparison to someone or something else. If you find someone at the office impressive or admirable in some way, you can and should tell them so. Just don't add a qualifier! They don't look nice today for an older person. They're not smart for someone with their background. It's not a surprise that they're knowledgeable about the issues for someone with their level of education. They're just attractive, or smart, or erudite. Period.

You can still say lots of things. You just can't do or say hurtful, ignorant things and expect no one to point out that it's ignorant or hurtful. And if you're really the nice person you think you are, you'll be grateful that someone did you the favor of pointing out when you screw up. A truly nice person would want to be told when there's a hole in their understanding so they're less likely to offend or disrespect anyone again. Thoughtful people evolve as their knowledge grows, and their language reflects that growth. It's why we don't still talk like first graders when we're 25.

If you find yourself feeling resentful that social mores have changed and that what was once acceptable or unremarkable no longer is, ask yourself why. Most likely, you'll find traces of fear and the scarcity mentality we discussed in Chapter 3. In addition, it's probable that your definition of what's "normal" is outdated and unreflective of a world that has expanded, matured, and become more inclusive. In general, most of this kind of anxiety, resentment, and fear can be resolved when you're brave enough to do the work that can bring you to a state of Radical Acceptance.

When you look back at history, you'll notice that the people who chafed and protested against change in favor of expanding rights and respect for people who didn't previously get much don't tend to come out looking very good. Is that who you want to be? Once you stop seeing the world in zero-sum terms, you'll find that you don't get irritated when you learn it's once again time to adopt a new vocabulary word or wrap your head around a foreign concept that didn't exist back in the day. Most of the time, all that's being asked of you is to think about how to be nicer to people. When that's the case, what have you got to lose?

There's an interesting coda to the story about the man who greeted me with the N-word. I'd lost my shit the night this dude insulted me, but upon reflection I did think it was important to find out what was going through his head that made him think he could speak that way to me. I reached out to him through a mutual acquaintance, and he agreed to meet me for coffee. The conversation was, in essence, a bias check. He tried to tell me that he had a close group of Black friends who let him talk like that around them all the time. They'd given him a pass. I let him know that his pass was not redeemable at all locations. I admit that I wouldn't have had the same reaction if a Black person had used that word with me. I wouldn't have liked it and would have asked them to stop, especially if it was someone I didn't know, but I would have known a Black person meant me no harm. From a white person, it's weaponized. The discussion around the N-word is emotionally charged and inspires an array of opinions. Mine is that it's a word no one should say. The rules of who can use it and when are too subjective and hard to fathom, and for many Black folks, it has too much blood and pain attached to it.

My hope was that he would walk away from our conversation with a new understanding of how people outside his biasphere might feel about this subject. I could have called him out on social media; I could have named his workplace and ruined his career. But I didn't want to cancel the guy; I just wanted to change his heart. And I think I did. When he apologized, he was in tears. He admitted he'd messed up and that what he'd said was wrong. I have to believe that he heard me and that he won't repeat his mistake. Everyone deserves a second chance.

You may think that means I don't believe in cancel culture, and you'd be right. Most of the time, anyway. For example, I think most people would want to know if they were working alongside individuals so bigoted they were compelled to participate in a march wearing Nazi insignia and chanting "Jews will not replace us." Companies would be within their rights to distance themselves from anyone with such ideology, not only to preserve their public image, but also out of respect for their other employees and to preserve a functioning work culture. In general, however, the consequences for people's bad decisions or behavior, especially in the social media age, should be handled on a case-by-case basis. Most people's errors stem from thoughtlessness and ignorance, not virulent bigotry and racism. Young people, especially, still have ample time to learn and change. I'd much rather give people a chance to grow and evolve than chase them into dark corners where their only company are others who willfully cling to BS that has no place in polite, respectful society, the types that need new recruits to make themselves feel better about their own poor choices. The punishment should match the transgression. Sometimes that means a person should be canceled or fired, but many times it doesn't. A more effective way to deal with BS-driven mistakes in the workplace than immediate firing would be through a form of restorative justice, in which the offender is held accountable for their error, then given a chance to learn more about the harm that error can cause, and to participate in efforts that help reverse or minimize the damage. If a company is built on a bedrock of Radical Acceptance, with all employees on board with the idea that everyone is a work in progress and creating a BS-free culture takes effort from all sides, it could work.

Look, I can make a hundred lists for you and teach you everything I know, and it's possible you're still going to do or say the one thing it never occurred to me I needed to tell you not to. I cannot protect you from every poorly thought-out word that comes out of your mouth or steer you away from a stupid impulse. The truth is, whether it's wishing strangers Merry Christmas when we have no idea if they're Christian or even celebrate the holiday, to assuming our gay co-worker wouldn't want to be invited to our Super Bowl party but asking everyone else on the team to come, every one of us can be insensitive at some time or another. All you can do is apologize. Don't deflect or deny, don't bullshit or make excuses. Just apologize. "I did something wrong, and I am so sorry." You'd be amazed at how well a true apology that accepts responsibility and asks for forgiveness will be received, mostly because it's such a rare thing to hear nowadays.

Six-time platinum certified singer Lizzo provided a perfect example of the kind of apology I'm talking about. When she released her song "Grrrls," the Internet went wild. At issue was one of the lyrics in which she referred to herself as a "spaz." As fans pointed out to her via tweets and Instagram, *spaz* is a slur used against people who've lost control of their muscles and coordination, short for "spastic." Within days, she released an unequivocal apology. "I never want to promote derogatory language," she tweeted. She didn't try to explain that she hadn't intended to harm. She didn't try to deflect blame. She wrote that she had listened to the criticism and complaints, and what she heard made her turn inward and realize she was perpetuating the same harm on others that was frequently perpetuated on her, a "fat, black woman in America." Finally, she decided that artistic integrity was less important than insulting an entire category of people and announced that she had released a new version of the song with a change in lyrics.

It's just a word, but as a songwriter, Lizzo knows better than anyone that words have extraordinary power to move people. As society evolves, so should our language. That's not caving in to wokeness or cancel culture. It's just being respectful.

When you've done the deep inner work from Part I of this book, you'll be far less likely to commit microaggressions. We can keep these hurtful moments under control by constantly checking our biases and assumptions, thinking before we speak, and putting ourselves in other people's shoes so we can try on a new perspective. Even so, sometimes they can be like toxic sludge seeping out from the depths of your psyche. You can plant a field of grass and daisies, and below the surface it could still be freaking Chernobyl. Knowing this, is there any other way, short of policing every word that comes out of your mouth, to disarm microaggressions? Yes, with micro-inclusions, actions you can take each day to ensure your colleagues feel a sense of acceptance and belonging.

RADICAL ACTS

Just as microaggressions are small, subtle comments and actions that make people feel ostracized or othered, micro-inclusions are small, subtle comments and acts of kindness that make people feel welcomed and give them a sense of belonging. They're not hard! In fact, many of them came naturally to you when you were five years old, before your BS got in the way.

One of the biggest, most impactful micro-inclusions you can make is smiling. Yes, just smiling at people in the hallway is an inclusive gesture. Everyone can do it, but the higher up the food chain you are, the stronger the impact. A woman who worked for a huge bank told me that her boss never smiled or said hello to her in the hall-way, ever, which made her feel like there was a problem—she just didn't know what it was. "I'm always walking on eggshells," she complained. It was impossible to relax and enjoy doing her work. She was especially sensitive to the chilly atmosphere because it was such a different vibe from where she'd worked before, a company run by a well-known wellness celebrity. She didn't see the celebrity much, but every time she did, she noticed that they would smile and greet every-one they saw in the room. Everywhere they went, they'd nod and ask how people's day was going. My friend's manager, taking her cue from the big boss, behaved much the same way.

My friend mused, "If somebody like that, with their busy schedule and level of celebrity, can come into a room and say hello and ask you how your day is and make you feel good about your role in the company, surely this guy can do it. And even if he can't, I can." To counteract the bank culture, she had started making a concerted effort to smile at people and wish them good morning when she got on the elevator. Even if they didn't reply, she felt good knowing that she was spreading positivity. Maybe she'd made someone feel a little better about coming in to work that day, even if she never found out about it.

Note that asking your team to make an effort to carry a pleasant demeanor at work and do their best to be welcoming and courteous with each other is not the same thing as telling women or girls who pass you by that they should smile more. Please don't do that. It's one thing to set the cultural tone at work. It's a whole other thing to make women feel like it's their job to be prettier for you or to make you more comfortable.

Other micro-inclusions you can try:

- Asking team members about their lives outside of work

- Pronouncing names correctly

- Being patient and present. That means taking the time to properly train people and communicate well. It also requires putting down the phone and making eye contact with whomever you interact with.

If it's in your purview:

- Extend opportunities for team members to grow and expand by instituting listening circles that allow colleagues to learn more about each other, including some of the tough things they endure at work. Also let coworkers know how they can be supportive of each other.

- Provide constructive criticism training, which teaches colleagues how to offer critique and bring out each other's best work without alienating, offending, or creating a toxic environment.

- Boost colleagues' ideas in meetings by throwing the conversation in their direction or directly asking for their opinions. When they speak, affirm your interest and ask them to elaborate. If someone has spoken to you in private or you hear about someone's idea outside the meeting, ask them to share their thoughts with the group. Make sure no one that is brave enough to speak is met with awkward silence.

- Offer to mentor the newest and youngest employees, as well as women and POC who don't have as many role models to draw from. Let co-workers who show potential know that you've noticed them. Talk to them about their future career plans and ask if they'd like you to help them reach their goals.

- Publicly acknowledge and celebrate people for their good work.

All these gestures will feel normal and easy when you've done the inner work outlined in Part I and commit to changing the culture by bringing your new radically aware and acceptant self to work. You do have the power to make change through something as simple as a smile or a simple conversation. We all do.

CHAPTER 8

RETHINKING THE RULES TO ACHIEVE EQUITY

Toward the end of a workshop in Austin, Texas, where'd I'd spent about an hour leading a small but engaged group through a series of thought exercises and discussions about confronting our BS and speaking up for diversity in the workplace, a woman of color sitting at a table in the back of the room threw up her hand. She was in a tough spot, she informed us. She'd been working at a company for several years and was losing patience with the BS she'd learned to expect from certain people in her workplace. She had more experience than most of the staff, yet she felt she had no voice. She was generally talked over or ignored when she brought up her ideas in meetings, only to hear those same ideas treated like gold when they were brought up five minutes later by someone else, usually a man. She felt conflicted because the younger, newer staff members sometimes turned to her for advice about how they could position themselves for success at the company, and she didn't know what to say. Should she tell them the truth, which was that if they were ambitious but female or BIPOC, they should probably start looking elsewhere? As she began, she spoke clearly and confidently, but then her voice hitched a little as she said, "I finally went to my supervisor to bring up a formal complaint and ask what I should do next, and she said she didn't know because the same thing was happening to her."

I was about to tell her she had a tough choice to make while also encouraging her to keep working on moving the needle if she chose to stay, when a Black man, also sitting in the back, spoke up. "Leave," he said emphatically. "Every company is putting policies in place to deal with this kind of thing and actively working to diversify its upper levels of power. If your company isn't even trying yet, it's a lost cause."

He was right. The woman's plight reminded me of the story I told in Chapter 5, about the time I presented to the CEO of a company who just sat there stony-faced, not even pretending to believe that one word that I was saying was important to him. He was never going to support change, and anyone at that company who continued trying to get him to was just going to burn out. Women and nonbinary members of the workforce are tired, and BIPOC are exhausted. Exhausted from wondering every day if they'll have to brace themselves for a microaggression, exhausted from trying to be heard, and from frequently being the only person who looks or sounds like them in a room. BIPOC women have the added stress of never knowing if the marginalization they experience is due to their race, gender, or both. They've done everything they can to succeed within the structures of the system as it currently stands. So now it's up to the people who hold those structures in place, the people in power, to start shouldering the burden of making change happen. If they choose not to, save yourself and preserve your energy for someplace where you actually can make a difference. Believe me, people are watching, especially the new generation of workers. If leaders and managers want to compete for the best talent and stem turnover, they have to show they're at least trying to make their company a place where that talent believes it can thrive. I don't expect to see those who refuse last much longer.

Much of what we've discussed in this book has been about how we can use Radical Acceptance to create change on a peer-to-peer level. But leaders and managers have the opportunity to do the same thing on a grand scale by setting policies, guidelines, and culture grounded in Radical Acceptance. That doesn't mean that if you're not at a managerial or executive level you can't get something out of this chapter. If you're familiar with what inclusive company policies should look like, you'll be better able to look for them when job hunting yourself. And if you like your current job, I hope this information prompts you to look over the policies and processes to see where your company is succeeding and where it could improve. It's like they say at the airport or on public transportation—if you see something, say something. Especially—and this is key—especially if you're a member of the dominant group. It's one thing for people directly affected by exclusionary policies to complain about them. Hell, they've been doing it for years. That's why it's so easy for people in power to tune them out. But as we've discussed, in an environment where the dominant group is the one that gets heard, it's up to members of the dominant group to push for change. We have to care about fixing harmful policies even when we're not the ones being harmed.

BUILD DEI INTO YOUR CULTURE

The company handbook lists the rules a company has decided must be met in order to meet goals and cultivate a connected culture. But do you really need these rules? As these rules have been updated over the years, have they really reflected changing mores and encouraged harmony, or do they actually maintain the status quo? I know some HR person may be reading this and getting nervous. Hold on, I'm not asking you to chuck all rules. I'm asking you to think differently about them and consider how they affect everyone who doesn't look like the rule makers. Now that you've learned how to be better than your BS, how can you rewrite the rules to build a company that's better too?

The obvious place to start would be setting up a DEI office and establishing an experienced DEI director or chief diversity officer to run the program. This department would be responsible for developing programs and services that promote and support inclusivity. Like HR, this department acts as a liaison between executives and staff, but until now HR hasn't usually been trained for DEI work (that may be changing). Too often companies try to move someone from HR into a newly created DEI position without making sure they have the proper education and tools to do the job well. Also, if you move someone over from HR, you have to be sure that the person has built relationships anchored in trust with diverse employees. Companies report that the number one barrier to implementing DEI is that the person in charge has neither the time nor authority to roll it out properly. In worst-case scenarios, DEI becomes a volunteer project, something added on to an employee's usual job. That employee, more often than not, is one of the few employees of color at the company. That's like finding a shipwreck survivor floating on a raft and asking them to tow their rescue boat to shore. Prove that you are committed to DEI and hire someone trained and qualified to usher your company into a newly diverse and radically accepting era.

Let's say you're a small business, however, or you're just starting out, and you can't invest in a formal DEI program. You can achieve similar results by writing or rewriting your employment rules and examining your communication channels through a DEI lens to ensure that diversity and allyship is baked into your business, and create comfortable work environments that encourage employees to speak up so they can help you achieve your DEI goals. They should be tied to your company goals. If so, you will see an increase from your productivity to your profits.

I was called in to conduct a policy review for a national organization that teaches financial literacy and entrepreneurship to young people from low-income communities. Given that the poverty rate among Black and Hispanic families is more than twice that of non-Hispanic white families,[1] the group's beneficiaries are largely racial minorities. With its focus on elevating the chances for diverse populations to succeed in the business world, you'd think this well-established company would have adopted some elements of DEI over the years to make sure it was making room for some of the members of those populations to establish careers with them. But it was hard to find any trace. What I found instead was a classic example of how neglecting DEI can hamstring the effectiveness and reach of companies committed to doing good. The solution was to focus a DEI lens on every aspect of their internal communications channels and public marketing content, then reconstruct them with DEI at their fulcrum. I offer you the same advice.

FOCUS A DEI LENS ON YOUR . . .
EMPLOYEE HANDBOOK

One exceedingly simple way to eliminate exclusive policies, and show people that your company prioritizes inclusivity, is to address the language you use in all of your internal and external communications. Most forward-looking companies have eliminated gendered language in theirs. That means instead of relying exclusively on binary gendered pronouns like *he/she* or *him/her*, they'll use the more gender-neutral *they*.

RADICAL ACT

Examine every policy through the eyes of a POC, LGBTQ+ person, and non-Christian. Better yet, ask employees from these groups to review the policies for you or set up a DEI task force for this express purpose. Asking your employees' opinion would have the added benefit of giving them a sense of ownership of the culture and help them feel invested in the success of the company.

Some people automatically reject the idea of gender-neutral pronouns. In fact, the city of Buenos Aires, Argentina, recently issued one of the world's first bans on gender-neutral language in schools.[2] The truth is, however, that all of us have been using these neutral pronouns forever. When an anonymous professional of any kind could just as likely be a woman as a man, we hedge our bets by referring to them as "they." "Have you called a lawyer? They might be able to help." It might take some getting used to when referring to a specific individual you know who looks to you like a cisgender woman or a man (someone whose gender identity matches the sex they were assigned at birth). I'll admit it wasn't easy for me. In the meantime, you can still make sure you use gender-neutral pronouns in your employee handbook and all other written text connected to your company. It may take your older workers a minute or two to train themselves to use these pronouns consistently, but they'll get there, and your newer, younger employees will take it for granted that this is how they're expected to write and talk when at work or attending off-site work functions.

Your employee handbook should include the following types of policies:

Belonging Policy

A belonging policy ensures that team members feel visible and appreciated. It's one thing to state your company's values in a Culture Commitment. It's a whole other level of Radical Acceptance to codify those values in a document like an employee handbook.

A sample belonging policy might say:

All employees are entitled to feel secure and supported by colleagues. All colleagues are required to make efforts to accept their co-workers' diversity, invite perspectives, and respect identities in work functions. Our company promotes the value of authenticity in the workplace because we believe when employees feel like they don't belong at work, their work performance and quality of life suffer. All employees are required to take actions that promote inclusion and foster belonging. Employees who promote these values will find themselves making intentional connections with those who are different, creating diverse teams that solve problems, providing mentorship to colleagues, inviting diverse perspectives into business operation decisions, and creating space for sharing personal narratives.

Zero-Tolerance Policy

A zero-tolerance policy is one that establishes a standard set of consequences for infractions that can't change at the discretion of who metes out the consequences or who is responsible for the infraction. It protects your company from any employee behavior or speech that is illegal, inappropriate, or fails to align with what's detailed in your organization's employee handbook.

You'd think that most adult employees would know what is considered appropriate behavior and speech in the workplace, and what isn't. But the need for zero-tolerance policies is real. I worked with a company who discovered one of their managers had incredibly poor judgment. While chatting with a company client, he shared an anecdote that had happened many years earlier in which a co-worker, while struggling to hang a picture in her office, casually claimed she'd have to "N-word-rig it" to get it to stay on the wall. The clients, who were understandably very uncomfortable during this exchange, told another contact at the company what had happened. The manager was fired immediately. Yet he couldn't understand why. He hadn't said the ugly word, he was just repeating what someone else had said. It was outrageous to fire someone for that! Except it wasn't. The company had a zero-tolerance policy against using racist language in any situation. It was right there in the employee handbook, where it expressly stated that the consequence for violating this policy was termination.

I've been doing this work for a long time, and yet I still manage to be surprised at what some people will think is okay to say or do in the workplace unless they are specifically informed they can't:

A friend of mine was hired to conduct sexual harassment training at a company where a zero-tolerance policy was implemented after one man was caught on camera following a female co-worker out of the building to her car, where he forcibly held her down and tried to kiss her, and another employee followed a woman to the bathroom, where he locked the door behind her and proceeded to try to feel her up and kiss her. My friend had to explicitly let men at this company know that feeling, touching, or kissing without consent would be a fireable offense.

Another company had to create a zero-tolerance policy to deal with people who would ask female employees if they were pregnant, and touch their stomachs without permission.

At another, a zero-tolerance policy was created to deal with a slew of theft and falsifying company documents.

Finally, in states where marijuana is legal, several companies have had to draft zero-tolerance policies against showing up high at work. Somehow people seem to remember that despite it being legal for adults to drink alcohol, being drunk at work is unacceptable. Yet that same common sense flies out the window when it comes to weed.

Zero-tolerance policies may seem excessive, but they can help set the tone at your workplace and make it clear to everyone, without a doubt, what's acceptable and what isn't.

Anti-Bullying Policy

Few zero-tolerance policies mention bullying, but they should. I always encourage my clients to include it.

I knew an employee at a large bank whose supervisor verbally bullied her and said such terrible things about her behind her back, the employee started recording conversations when she would leave her desk to go to the bathroom and other places where the supervisor didn't suspect she was being overheard. When the employee went to HR with the recordings, HR was more concerned about the legality of recording someone without their knowledge (it was legal in that state) than they were about the supervisor's vicious backbiting language. Instead of dealing with the problem, they moved the employee to a different department. Meanwhile, the supervisor remained in her job.

Early in my career, when I owned a diversity communications firm but before I started speaking, a client called me for help when Black employees threatened to sue if they didn't put a stop to a string of racist events at the company, including someone repeatedly leaving nooses hanging from the ceiling and pictures of tar babies on Black employees' desks. The company didn't want to be perceived by its employees or anyone else that it condoned this behavior, yet they didn't take any action until the Black employees hired one of the top discrimination lawyers in the nation to represent them. They settled out of court. I was brought in to help boost Black employee morale. It seemed to me that the best way to boost morale was for leadership to prove it was pulling out all the stops to turn around what was clearly a corrosively racist culture (these events had happened repeatedly, and someone had to know who was behind them yet had never stepped forward to make them stop), but the most they offered was some new sensitivity training, the kind of inexpensive one-and-done CYA workshops that can shield a company from scrutiny and lawsuits. At the time DEI officers or departments weren't common, and no rewriting of policy, no culture audit, and no change in recruiting or hiring practices was ever considered. It was one of the cases that edged me firmly toward reinventing myself as a diversity trainer. I had zero interest in boosting morale at a company whose executives were doing nothing to solve the issues dragging down morale in the first place.

No one should have to secretly record bullying in order to be believed, and the answer shouldn't be to move the employee out of the bully's line of sight because there will always be someone else for the bully to target. It shouldn't take a lawsuit to put an end to racist aggression in the workplace. Both companies could have avoided a lot of drama and potential legal trouble if they'd set up a zero-tolerance bullying policy from the outset.

The youth organization didn't have one, and we stressed that without it they were vulnerable to the exact same kind of problems and threats as these other companies. They will work if they're enforced. When there's a policy in place meant to protect them if they speak out against bullying, and they are confident there will be repercussions if that accusation can be supported, employees report problematic language and behavior. If policies are on the books, but there are no consequences when bullying is brought to light, employees lose confidence and trust in you and the company, and bullies are empowered. This is often how toxic work environments are born.

Anti-Retaliation Policy

This one protects employees from reprisals if they file a claim or grievance against a co-worker or other employee, including through HR. It's necessary because sometimes managers, supervisors, or other individuals with power over an employee can hinder their career trajectory in the form of a lost promotion, a demotion, or pay inequity.

Fear of retaliation can have a severe chilling effect on people's ability to advocate for themselves. During an IDI, a woman confided that she'd been trying to get her partner benefits for years, ever since the company began offering benefits to same-sex partners. She kept filling out the paperwork and had repeatedly called HR to find out what was holding things up, but one manager in the department consistently gave her the runaround, and mysteriously, her paperwork kept disappearing or getting stalled. I asked the woman why she didn't go over the manager's head and contact the head of HR in the corporate office, who I happened to know was a terrific person who would have immediately rectified the situation. The woman shared that she had heard from other employees that this particular HR manager had a nasty reputation, and there was talk she'd gotten people she didn't like fired or demoted in the past. The employee was worried about losing her job. She and her partner had a baby, and she was the only one working. Her plan was to find a new job and file a complaint during her exit interview.

I asked her to trust me. I, too, had a partner, and what was happening to her was horrible. Would she give me a chance to help her? She agreed, and as soon as her interview was over, I called the head of HR and told her what was happening. As I predicted, she was appalled and stunned, and immediately got everything in order to get this woman her benefits. Later, I received an e-mail from her profusely thanking me for my help, and as far as I know she never suffered any consequences for going over the HR manager's head. Still, it wasn't something she should ever have had to fear. Had an anti-retaliation policy been in place, she would have had the freedom to speak her mind and gotten her problem solved years earlier.

Dispute Resolution Policy

You'll need a plan in place to guide participants when it's necessary to bring two sides together to examine a cause of friction. It will be important to make it clear ahead of time that the conversation won't shy away from exposing racism or any other "ism" if that's what's at the heart of the problem. And as uncomfortable as this type of mediation can be, you'll find that it's better to call things out for what they are, because that's when you really have the opportunity to nudge people to open up their perspectives and change.

Dress Code

Throughout this book we've drawn attention to marginalizing, discriminatory policies, such as policies that restrict how women can wear their hair, that label any clothing or hairstyles that veer from traditionally straight, white standards as "unprofessional." Interestingly, the youth organization had the most antiquated dress code I've ever seen. Of course the employees and representatives of a group dedicated to teaching young people how to succeed in business should serve as role models, which would include showing kids what classic business attire looks like and teaching them how to dress appropriately for professional events. But not all or even most employees had direct contact with kids, and even if they did, the business world has moved on since the 1980s, which is when this dress code might have been written. Women could wear pants, but only classic trousers. (I would love for someone to explain to me what classic trousers are.) They were limited to business-appropriate jewelry, which I'm still struggling to define. There were rules about what kind of shoes men and women could wear. Men were required to wear ties, keep their hair cut short, and keep their face clean-shaven. I've seen banks with more relaxed dress codes.

As we explained to our client, at this point it will be hard to get Millennials and Gen Z to consider working for companies that don't offer flexible remote work options; forcing them into heels or a tie every day puts up unnecessary barriers between you and the talent you want to reach. In addition, hewing to such strict gender-based clothing rules announces loud and clear to nonbinary folks that your company is someplace that's going to make it difficult for them to show up as themselves. Young people communicate their personalities and preferences through their clothes. Our recommendation was that the employees of an organization invested in connecting with young people should be allowed to do the same. And the restriction against facial hair? That's like putting up a sign that says, "No Muslims or Orthodox Jews allowed." It was a lawsuit waiting to happen.

If at this point you're still concerned about making sure your employees project a "professional" appearance, turn back to Chapter 4, Redefining Normal. Where do your ideas about what counts as a "professional" look come from, exactly? Who in your mind looks "professional"?

Mental Health Days

At my office, we check in frequently with each other to see how everyone is holding up. If I find out someone is feeling overwhelmed or, as we like to call it, snapping their crayons, I encourage them to take a mental health day. My employees know they'll get no judgment from me if they need to take some time to get their shit together. I want my employees feeling strong so they can be productive and creative when they're on the job. Most people reading this book will likely already receive sick leave. A company that offers and normalizes mental health days does a lot to set themselves apart and signals they are up to date and delivering best practices to employees and consumers alike. Make it explicit that it is fine to use a sick day as a mental health day.

Continued Education

Ensure every employee receives opportunities for continued education and upward mobility and make it easy for employees to take time off to participate in workshops and attend classes that will make them more valuable and productive for you.

Website

Create a diversity tab so that anyone interested can easily find the data that proves you're not just talking about diversity and inclusion, but actively working on it. For example, here you would list what percentage of your employees are female, POC, and LGBTQ+, as well as what percentage work at all levels.

RADICAL ACT

Many large companies like Apple, Microsoft, and Google are publishing annual diversity reports so the public can see their progress. Taking a strong stance like this shows you're serious about creating an inclusive and equitable workplace.

Regardless of whether these numbers look good or not, use this opportunity to outline everything you're actively doing to maintain the parity you've achieved or rectify the imbalances. This is also where you should post your Culture Commitment. One space-saving idea would be to select a particularly powerful quote from that document and provide the option to click to read the document in its entirety.

Recruitment Strategy

When we asked employees at the youth organization what would make them feel confident that their company was really working to diversify and promote inclusion, the number one answer was they wanted to see changes to the recruiting process. The company had a lot of women working for it, including in high-level roles. But with one or two exceptions, the company was lily white. This in a company with chapters across the country. This in a company whose primary focus is reaching out to, connecting with, and elevating Black and brown kids.

Offering ideas for how the company could reach more diverse recruits turned out to be easy because they actually had no recruitment strategy in place. Never in my 25-year career had I encountered a company that hadn't put at least one page together nominally stating how and where they would fish for new hires. But here we were, starting from scratch.

Typically, a natural place to recruit is from local universities. Every year these institutions pump out a new crop of young, energized graduates ready to put what they've learned in the classroom into real-world practice. Which local universities, though? Most of the time, companies target the same few, which are usually the big, well-known universities in the area completely ignoring small community and historically Black colleges and universities (HBCUs). On most university campuses you'll find women's groups, AAPI groups, LGBTQ+ groups, and Black Student Government groups. There are plenty of professional organizations to reach out to as well, no matter what your field, from the National Association of Asian American Professionals, to the National Society of Black Engineers (NSBE), to the Society for the Advancement of Chicanos and Native Americans in Science, to the Association for Women in Mathematics (AWM). We urged our clients to advertise to these groups and develop strong relationships with them to create candidate pipelines for jobs and internships.

We also urged them to up their social media game, which is something we have to tell most of our clients. If you take the time to gain cultural competency, establish yourself as an expert in your field, and use the right hashtags, you open up opportunities to engage in conversations with individuals that could be excellent matches for your company. A robust social media presence will make you noticeable to anyone in your field looking for work or hoping to make a change. Give your ideal candidates a reason to click to your website and learn more about why they should want to work with you.

Hiring

Note that you can take all the steps listed above and publicly proclaim the most inclusive policies imaginable, and if you don't follow them up with process and action, your employees will reveal the truth. It takes a combination of implementing the policies listed above, plus leading inclusively, plus hiring employees that are self-aware of their isms and unconscious bias (or educating employees to become so) to create a connected culture. If all your efforts are merely performative, you'll see it in your retention rates and difficulties in hiring diverse candidates.

As you diversify your recruitment strategies, you'll want to be sure you have policies in place that ensure an equitable hiring process. Researchers have found that unless hiring requirements are well established before interviews begin, employers will unconsciously allow their BS to shift their priorities and erect barriers that help candidates they like and justify refusing candidates they don't. Once those hiring requirements are set in stone, however, the BS is kept to a minimum and a larger number of diverse candidates are hired.[3]

I was called in to work with the counseling department of a prestigious university that had been struggling to coalesce and cooperate ever since one particular hiring decision. A Black woman had been the preferred candidate for a new position, but one member of the department, a white woman, had worked with the Black woman ten years earlier when they were both starting out their careers.

"She wasn't very good," was the department member's assessment. "Unprofessional." Yet in the ten years since, the candidate had racked up impressive accomplishments and credentials, and she came highly recommended. The eight other counselors on the hiring team—seven white, one Black—thought that on paper this Black candidate looked perfect for the job, but the white woman who had worked with her a decade earlier stood her ground and continued to insist, with no evidence and only her memory of events that took place ten years prior, that the Black woman wasn't really "professional." The white woman had a strong personality, and eventually the other department members caved, even the lone Black member who all along had continued to fight for the Black woman's candidacy. No one ever mentioned the candidate's race, but with so little to go on other than one woman's hazy recollection of "unprofessional" behavior a decade before, it was hard not to suspect unconscious racism at play.

By the time I was called, the group could barely function. There was nothing to be done—the event had happened months before—so the best I could do was draw attention to the fact that had the specific requirements for the job been agreed upon ahead of time, the rejected candidate would at least have gotten an interview and a chance to let the board make their own first impressions, as well as perhaps speak to the concerns of the one member who didn't even want to give her a chance. I asked how many people in the group thought they were as good at their jobs ten years ago, or at the beginning of their careers, as they were today. That's when someone muttered, "We really messed up." The Black woman started crying tears of relief and said, "Thank you. Thank you so much for acknowledging that the way this decision was handled was wrong." On one hand, she'd felt incredible pressure to help a member of her community get a fair shot at a good job, and on the other, she'd been concerned about protecting her own position. It's the rock and hard place between which a large number of BIPOC find themselves in by virtue of usually being the only member of their group in the room. The Black woman's tears got another colleague crying. It was a shit show, but at least some healing began. At least, among the eight board members who recognized that they'd allowed themselves to be swayed by one insistent voice. That woman, the one who'd blocked the Black woman's candidacy, never seemed to understand what was wrong with her line of thinking and was peeved that she even had to revisit the issue.

Once you do determine your nonnegotiable hiring requirements, be careful that you don't let them hold excellent candidates at arm's length. For example, there's a lot of debate about whether a college degree should remain the standard requirement that it has become. For some jobs, a degree, and possibly an advanced degree, is necessary. But are four-year degrees really necessary for all the jobs at your company? Sometimes it's the person with more life experience than academic credentials who's the perfect fit for the position you need to fill. Be careful that your recruitment materials don't discourage people with the exact skills and talents you need and keep an open mind when scheduling interviews. An older worker who's been around the block a few times may require much less hand-holding and training than a young person with little life experience but a fancy degree. For example, a client we were working with needed more men on their staff. Yet the majority of college campuses skew female today, some 40 to 60 percent. On top of that, many people who become entrepreneurs don't go to college or drop out to pursue their passion right away. By requiring college degrees, this organization was limiting its ability to bring more men into the fold. They needed to redefine their normal and ask themselves, what's more important for teaching kids about business and entrepreneurialism, a college degree or experience running a business and being an entrepreneur? Whether you're hiring for one position or many, you want to draw from the biggest pool of talent possible. With Radical Acceptance and the recruitment strategies mentioned above in place, you'll have one.

Ideally, hiring shouldn't be left to just one or two people, but to a diverse panel representing people of different races, genders, and if possible, even physical abilities. This does slow the hiring process down, since it requires that each panel member be allowed to ask their own questions, get to know the candidates, and debate among themselves over who would be the better pick. But the results speak for themselves—companies wind up with a richer variety of skill sets and perspectives, which leads to more creativity, better innovation, and a more interesting workplace. In addition, a panel representing diversity can help put a lot of people's minds at ease when they can see that they won't be the only person who looks or sounds like them at the company.

During speaking engagements and keynotes, I use a tool that allows attendees in the audience to anonymously answer questions that are built into my presentation, such as, "What were you taught to reject about others?" It gives people the opportunity to be perfectly honest about their thoughts without fear of judgment. It also allows me to dig into some of the more egregious issues and deal with them on the spot.

RADICAL ACT

Use an online tool (such as Menti) to answer preloaded questions and assess a candidate immediately after the panel interview while people's impressions are still fresh. Ideally someone trained in DEI would be involved and able to guide a discussion to any answers that reveal bias, discrimination, or irrational, prejudiced thoughts so they could be dealt with and discarded. If someone has concerns about a candidate's age, weight, or their gold tooth, it comes out. Once they're aired everyone realizes how mean and middle-schooly they sound. Ask the important questions: Why does it matter how old this person is? Are your judgments rooted in evidence? How would someone's relatively advanced age affect this candidate's ability to perform the duties of their job? In my experience, once people see how irrational and prejudiced their thoughts are, they're able to push them aside and focus exclusively on the candidate's résumé and interview skills, which is the only thing that should have mattered in the first place. In this way, each hiring event not only gives candidates an equitable chance at a job, but also becomes a learning opportunity and an occasion to put Radical Acceptance at the center of the hiring process.

Many people will express fear that diversifying inevitably means passing over white men in the hiring process. No. Just no, it doesn't. What it does mean is that one of the qualifications of your ideal candidate is the ability to work well within this new diverse environment. Is the white person you're considering emotionally intelligent? Can they run a diverse team and validate people's experiences? Are they excited about coming up with innovative ways to grow this new world you're creating? Are they willing to listen, learn, and stay up to date with the latest in DEI research and best practices? By all means, hire them!

Prominently featuring these standards and policies on public-facing communication channels and internal documents like the handbook signals to prospective and new employees that your company is a safe environment. It also primes the pump so that whoever chooses to join the company is in the right mindset to help push the culture forward. Any new recruiter should know long before their first day that they'll need to bring diverse candidates to the hiring table. For many, it will be the first time they've been asked to do so. It serves as a prompt that should already be thinking more expansively about where they could tap into a larger, more diversified pool of possible talent. If you repeat that process over and over across departments so that everyone who comes in is committed to the same cause, your company will quickly start to look, sound, and perform differently.

Once these parameters and foundations are set, the people who can't figure out how to adapt or accept the rules will most likely leave on their own. That's okay, because the same policies that chase away people unwilling to evolve will attract new employees who are comfortable and maybe even comforted and energized by your policies.

ESTABLISHING EQUITY

When I first started this work, the talk was all about D&I, diversity and inclusion. Today, we talk about DEI—diversity, equity, and inclusion. Why? Because even when we achieve diversity and inclusion, it's for naught if we don't work toward equity.

Consider this example: let's say an adult professional is offered the opportunity to take a continuing education course. They have a hearing impediment. When they get to class, the only available seat is in the back of the room. The trainer is aware that this student can't hear well, but in the interest of treating everyone equally, refuses to move them to the front of the room. The trainer has good intentions, but they're not treating everyone with equity, because from the back of the room the student with hearing challenges will have a harder time keeping up than their peers who can clearly hear no matter where they sit. They got access to the same resources—same type of chair, same room, same trainer—as their hearing peers, but due to circumstances beyond their control, they can't fully use them. The equitable solution is to move them to the front of the room where they can hear the lessons and have the same opportunity as everyone else to benefit from instruction and engage with the trainer.

What would you think of anyone who complained about the student's "special treatment," or that they were taking a spot that rightfully belonged to a non-hearing-impaired person? It sounds selfish and callous, doesn't it? You'd expect anyone with an ounce of maturity to understand that someone with a disadvantage should be given the support they need to perform at their best.

That's what the proposals and policies in this chapter will achieve. Once you've pulled them all together—an inclusive website, recruitment strategy and hiring strategy; a robust employee handbook; a non-sexist, inclusive dress code; and solid, trustworthy feedback channels, among everything else—you're on your way to creating equity. An equitable system is one that grants people all the tools they need to succeed on their own initiative, with standard benchmarks for diversity and inclusion that offer employees an easy way to communicate their concerns, report on their work experience, and share their ideas. If we want to have the best teams, we need to give them the best tools to succeed. That's how we let people live up to their potential.

I coached basketball for years, and what I learned is that a coach can make the worst team the best team, and the best team the worst team. I learned that when you care about kids and are willing to go above and beyond for them, they'll give you their best. I knew which kids I could yell at, which kids I had to encourage with a warm hug, which ones needed me to go out on the court and demonstrate how I wanted things to be done. I take that same approach into the office with me. It takes more time, but it takes even more time to rebuild a team every time someone leaves. When you take the time to know your people, you can coach them to success. A team that trusts each other is a team that's willing to pull out all the stops to meet its goals. That trust can start building from the first minute a prospective employee comes into contact with you, online or in person.

CHAPTER 9

STAND BY ME

Creating Connected Culture through Allyship

> I just wanted you to know that I'm thinking about you and your family today. I've been catching up on the news, and I'm horrified about what is going on in our country. It is causing me a great deal of pain, so I can only imagine how it is making you feel.

> I've been thinking about you this week, obviously. How are you?

> This has upset me, made me angry, made me cry, and made me want to protect my students and educate them. I feel I don't know effective ways to end this situation of unarmed men of color being killed while other armed people are taken into custody unharmed. Sorry I am writing to you because I want to effectively help you stay safe. Love you.

These are actual text messages I received in June 2020 after the killing of George Floyd, sent by my white friends. Millions of other Black people received a similar outpouring. At first, I was indifferent. Prior to George Floyd, there was no outrage, and there should have been. There was also Breonna Taylor, Terence Crutcher, Eric Garner, Sandra Bland, Michael Brown, and 13-year-old Tamir Rice. Say their names. And yet none of my white friends had. Not to me, anyway. Just three months earlier, after running 2.23 miles, the distance mirroring the date Ahmaud Arbery was chased down and shot by white men unhappy that he was jogging through their neighborhood, I'd written an anguished post on Facebook: "When will this stop? When will we all stand up? It's not enough for Black people to stand. We're always standing, protesting, hurting, crying out. We know it doesn't matter. White folk constantly ask me what they can do or what they should be doing. You should be actively speaking and standing up . . . !" Few white people responded. Their sudden epiphany after the death of George Floyd felt like too little, too late.

But then I leaned in to Radical Acceptance. These were people I love and who love me. I could be upset that it had taken so much time to awaken their outrage, but I had to get over it. Because they were here. They'd finally listened, and they were validating a part of the Black American experience. Now I had to wait and see, would they act? They would. One joined the board of a Black-led nonprofit dedicated to raising awareness about and preserving the legacy of Oklahoma's all-Black towns (13 remain of the original 50).[1] From her position as an educator and organizer, she makes a big effort to make sure that when historical events are taught, the whole story is taught, not just the version passed down by the "winners," who are too often also oppressors. Another friend works at the executive level within a company and has made it a habit of thinking and leading inclusively. Another, a public speaker who focuses on leadership, invited me on her podcast so we could have an open conversation about why I was so angry. She's making a real effort to be more vocal both online and off about matters of race and inclusivity. Neither of these examples reflect grand gestures that prove solidarity, but they don't need to. All it takes is committing to keeping these issues top-of-mind and doing what one can within one's sphere of influence. My friends' small gestures let people know where they stood and modeled how those who care about this topic can show where they stand too.

It wasn't just my white friends and acquaintances who stood up. According to Stanford sociologist Douglas McAdam, since 2014, when Michael Brown was killed in Ferguson, MO, there had always been protests following the deaths of Black people at the hands of the police, but "overwhelmingly in the black community."[2] After George Floyd, between 15 and 26 million people in the U.S. participated in demonstrations, marking the largest protest movement in U.S. history. Protests cropped up in 40 percent of the counties in the U.S. Ninety-five percent of them were majority white, with white people making up over 75 percent of the population in about three-quarters of them.[3] White women, in particular, made a dramatic scene, more than once linking their arms together to protect Black bodies from the police. The three men shot by Kyle Rittenhouse at a Black Lives Matter protest—two of them fatally, both of them unarmed—were white. Part of the reason for the increase in numbers was that people had more free time to participate in protests because they were working from home or even unemployed because of the COVID-19 pandemic, and all other regular activities were on hold. But even as vaccines were rolled out and life started to resume normal rhythms, a large swath of people seemed to finally understand that just feeling sorry about the state of things wasn't enough. Change requires action, and until white people, straight people, and members of other dominant groups speak up and take action against indignities toward marginalized others, nothing changes. We saw it during the Civil Rights Movement, when the photo of poor Emmett Till's battered face, and later, TV images of police officers turning dogs and firehoses against children in Birmingham and state troopers clubbing peaceful marchers on the Edmund Pettus Bridge, turned the majority of public opinion in favor of desegregation and unfettered voting rights for all. We saw it during the Holocaust, when non-Jews joined resistance movements across occupied Europe, hid Jews in their homes, and passed Jewish children off as their own. We even saw it during the AIDS crisis, when a 34-year-old white, straight, wealthy mother of two named Mary Fisher spoke publicly about her HIV status at the 1992 Republican convention and urged her party and all Americans to reconsider their often cruel and bigoted attitude toward AIDS patients. She knew she broke the stereotype and that as a white conservative woman, she had the power to affect other conservatives' hearts and minds. There's no way to know if she would have stood up for AIDS victims had she not become HIV positive herself, but as she has defied the medical odds, she continues to this day to use her platform to inspire others to stand up, serve, and help even when they could say, "Not my fight." In 1994, she delivered a speech in Louisville, Kentucky, that's as relevant today as it was then:

Now and again someone sees the truth. A man comes by who hears the cries of an Argentine child, imprisoned for her parents' politics, being tortured by her jailers. "It could be my child," says the man, and he launches a crusade toward justice. Or a man on campus is held down in the shower room and abused with a broom handle by a laughing football team because he is gay until one of you rises up to say, "It could be my brother." In such moments, the spirit of ethics is no faint abstraction. It is a blindingly clear reality, a demanding plea, a cry you must answer . . .[4]

The acts you take don't have to be big, daring, or dangerous (read about Oskar Schindler, the Grimké sisters, Andrew Goodman and Michael Schwerner, and Viola Liuzzo, among others, who risked and sometimes lost everything standing up for justice even though it wasn't "their fight"). They can be small gestures of kindness, welcome, acknowledgment, and inclusion. They can encompass public pressure campaigns in the form of e-mails, social media statements, consumer boycotts, and what author Tanja Hester calls wallet activism. Anything to encourage companies to implement programs to dismantle their culturally baked in biases or ramp up the DEI programs they already have. And the pressure has to come from within the company as well. It makes a huge statement when it's no longer only the BIPOC or female or trans employees complaining about exclusive policies or actively pointing out ostracizing behavior from managers. When the noise makers look and sound like them, decision makers pay attention. This is not an issue that BIPOC, LGBTQ+, or religious minority communities can solve on our own. If we could, we'd have done it already. We need allies.

WHAT ALLYSHIP LOOKS LIKE

Long before I knew what an ally was, I had one in my cousin Pete. When I was little, my older cousins were put in charge of me every day while the grown-ups worked. Since they loved to play basketball, I had to play basketball. But they didn't actually teach me to play, and as I was younger and smaller than all of them, I was basically just a little body running around behind everyone on the court. I may as well have been playing hot potato for the amount of time my hands spent on the ball, since on the rare occasion I touched it, the other kids would start screaming at me to pass it. I quickly figured out that if I was ever going to learn how to play the game, I would have to teach it to myself. Mind you, I didn't like the sport. Who would with an introduction like that? But that was irrelevant. I was determined that one day I'd show them I could do what they said I couldn't.

I started getting up extra early so I could be the first kid in the gym and get some time alone on the court. Shortly after, another cousin started spending time at our gym. Pete was the coolest. Not only was he older than all of us, but he was also one of the best players in the state. I'd be stumbling around on one end of the court, and he'd be hanging with his boys on the other. One day he looked over and yelled out, "Hey, that's not how you shoot the ball! You do it like this." He walked over and informed me that the power to make the ball reach the net was in my legs, not my arms. "You want to shoot with your legs, and guide with your arms." Then he showed me what to do. Suddenly, BOOM! I could make the ball reach the goal!

From then on, every day when I showed up in the gym early in the morning, Pete was there too, waiting for me. It wasn't always easy. There were some days I thought I'd never master the form he was trying to teach me. He patiently listened to my frustrations, but he didn't give up on me. I got better fast, though it would take years of practice to consistently make my shots. Before I knew it, though, I was in love with the sport that I'd once hated.

Now, if you've ever played basketball, you know that at the end of the day when the older kids show up to play, all the younger ones have to leave. That is the law of the gym. One evening I started trailing off the court as the big kids were congregating, when this superstar cousin told me to stay put. Then he chose me to be on his team. I couldn't believe it. In my world, there was no higher honor. The older boys weren't just surprised, they were pissed. No one wanted to share their game with a skinny little girl. They talked shit to my cousin, but he held firm.

I gave that game everything I had, and Pete was there to make sure no one on my own team sabotaged my chance to shine. He passed me the ball when no one else would. When my teammates would try to take the ball away from me as usual, Pete would block them while actively coaching me. "Take the shot, Risha! Do it like I showed you!" If I made the shot, he would act like it was a really big deal, then talk noise to the other players because I had just scored. He validated my efforts and showed everyone he believed in me. I was so happy and proud I think I could have flown that day if I'd thought to try. Because I wasn't just allowed on the court, but also taught to play the game, I gained skills that I was able to parlay into several Division 1 scholarship offers. Allyship can be life-changing for the person who needs it.

Allyship is one of the most important catalysts for inclusion and creating connected culture. Inclusion is about doing everything we can to make sure people know they belong and feel welcome in a space. It's about noticing where barriers still exist, taking them down, and creating opportunities for people who have usually been marginalized to make themselves heard and seen. It's when we link arms, speak out on behalf of each other, and make clear where we stand. At your office, there are people who never speak up. Is it because they're shy, or is it because your organizational culture has showed them that they don't matter? You need to know, and if it's the latter, you can show them otherwise, just like my cousin showed me.

THREE RADICAL ACTS TO BEING A GOOD ALLY

Radical Act #1—Listen

Pete only intended to give me some pointers when he walked over to show me how to shoot, but then he took the time to listen deeply when I shared my frustrations. By asking the appropriate questions, he quickly figured out what he could do to help. In the office, you might just ask your colleague straight up how you can best help them feel like they belong and are part of the team. Strategize ideas together that would help address the situation.

Remember that you learned about deep listening in Chapter 6. Biasphere checks are an excellent way to find out what people are thinking and feeling, so long as you're listening to understand, not listening to respond. Also fortunately, thanks to social media and podcasts, we live in an era when you don't even have to talk to anyone in order to hear what the people in a community have to say about issues in real time. Finally, there are thousands of memoirs and works of gripping nonfiction that not only give you access to stories and examples of real-life allyship, but also frequently include insight into why individuals chose to step up. In the Break Down Your BS Resource Guide at the end of this book, you will find a list of books, television shows, movies, social media, and podcasts representing different experiences and points of view that may offer education, inspiration, and insight.

As you expand your search beyond those suggestions, you may become exposed to ideas and emotions that feel intimidating or even off putting to someone new to these conversations. You might be surprised or uncomfortable with how angry some people are. I urge you to stick with them. There will be some with whom you disagree, and that's fine. You'll also want to weed out the trolls and bots who engage on these sites and bring out the ugly in people, but that's easy to do—check when the profile was created and how many followers they have; if it was recently brought online and there are few to any followers, that profile is just there to cause trouble and spread misinformation and lies. Of course, there are real humans who get a kick out of doing the same, and you'll want to take what they say with a grain of salt as well. But if you pay attention to the vetted content creators on this list and focus on the rational, reasonable discussions and debates they get into, you'll start to understand where people not like you are coming from, and what they actually want and need from you.

Radical Act #2—Validate

Pete could have dismissed my frustration as the rantings of an angry little girl who sucked at playing basketball.

Instead, he took me seriously, and in doing so showed me that I wasn't alone or powerless. You can earn a lot of goodwill and trust by simply acknowledging the reality of a situation from people who are accustomed to being ignored. If a colleague complains about a persistent problem, you could answer, "I'm so sorry that happened. I've heard of situations like this before. Let's figure out what we can do to make it better or who we need to talk to in order to change things." Make clear you're not acting out of pity or trying to be patronizing. Rather, this is about wanting to benefit from the whole team's talent and ideas.

When talking to people or asking about their perspectives, be humble. Express empathy. Confirming the reality of a situation and conveying the message, "I hear you, and regardless of how I feel, I see that it bothers you and I'm willing to do what it takes to help," is an important way of letting people know you care.

Radical Act #3—Take Action

After learning about my problem and realizing he was in a position to do something about it, Pete . . . did something about it. Allies look for every opportunity to act. Smile at people and ask them how they're doing—and stick around to hear the answer! Speak up when you hear something problematic. If you're able to offer someone visibility on a project, do it. Help people find their voice by bringing up their idea in meetings and asking them to further share. Give credit to the correct people. If you're in a meeting and you hear a man receive praise for and interest in an idea that a woman suggested earlier to general indifference, you can speak up. "Sarah just said something similar a minute ago, and I agree it's a great idea. Sarah, would you like to share more of your thoughts?" This is how you amplify others' voices and open up spaces to people who have previously felt locked out. Use your voice.

My cousin not only welcomed me onto the basketball court, but he also instilled in me confidence that I could have what I wanted if I went for it. He was the person who spent the most time with me in the beginning, but when my other cousins saw that I was improving and could even keep up, they started encouraging me and working with me too. They stopped chasing me off the court, and even shared their knowledge and skills with me. Pete took action, and in doing so, he inspired the other cousins to change their behavior toward me. Their biaspheres were such that it probably hadn't ever occurred to them to behave in any other way toward a skinny little girl trying to learn their game. It took watching someone they respected doing things differently to help them see things in a different light.

By the time I was a senior in high school, I earned several Division I scholarship offers. I'm proud of that, yet I know I have Pete, my other cousins, and my dad to thank. Not one of us got where we are by ourselves, even if we want to think we did. Yes, I was the one who spent all that time alone on the court at 6 A.M. working on my skills, and yes, I took the initiative to run down the middle of the street every day dribbling with one hand tied behind my back. These are things I chose to do to improve and build my skill. But it would have been for nothing if no one had ever taken the time to show me just how good I could get and then given me a chance to play. Not just in basketball, but in business too.

As a former athlete, I know your success is on you. Personal drive and responsibility are key to getting anywhere in life. But as long as we're all functioning within a system that's not set up to allow everyone equal access to opportunity, it's on us to stay aware of the moments when we can set things right and help someone step forward. If I'm on a team, whether as a leader or a member, I want everyone on that team to feel part of that team and to function at their strongest, because that's how we all rise.

Sometimes allyship has nothing to do with fostering teamwork, at least not directly. Sometimes being an ally is as simple as letting people know you see and appreciate them just the way they are, which ultimately makes them a happier, more secure, more productive human. My sister did that for me.

After my first sexual experience with a woman, I spent the next day crying and convinced my life was ruined. We hadn't planned it. There was no flirting. No conversation. No alcohol. It just happened. Something had pulled us together at the exact same time, and though we were both raised as Christians, in that moment we ignored what we'd been taught to believe about people like ourselves and the grave risks to our souls if we broke what we'd been told were the spiritual and moral rules of life.

The self-help gurus in books and on television promised some kind of mystical self-actualization once you were brave enough to reach out for what you wanted, but I wasn't feeling anything but self-loathing. Maybe my problem was that, until then, I didn't even know I wanted it. Nobody ever talked about the anxiety. The fear. The shock and disbelief of not being who you thought you were.

As the days turned into weeks and the weeks into months, I had a fleeting thought of not wanting to live anymore but I quickly nixed that. My next thought was to move as far away from my friends and family as possible after college. I had cried every day since the "incident" and my mom was worried about me. Normally I'm very open with her, and whenever I'm down or worried about something, at the sound of her voice I break down and tell her everything. For this reason, I kept my distance. Of all the things that she thought could be going on, I'm sure that me having an intimate relationship with a woman wasn't one of them. But I was scared. I was scared of the intimacy I felt with this woman, which I'd never felt with a man. I finally understood what all the R&B love songs were getting at. I'm not just talking about the pleasures of sex; I mean everything that all the Hallmark movies and romance novels tell you is possible with another person. I finally had it. Yet scarier than that was the thought that my parents, grandparents, and extended family might disown me. I knew they loved me, but there was no doubt they loved God more. And I'd been told that according to Him, same-sex relationships were an abomination. I didn't want to embarrass my family, and how would my grandparents face the other church folks in my small town if my secret got out? As I tried to pray the gay away daily, I was spiraling into a depressing and desolate space.

Then, my phone rang. It was my little sister. We've always been close. To this day, we've never been mad at each other for more than 24 hours. We have fought and argued like most siblings, but we are down for each other like four flat tires.

I answered the phone, trying to act like everything was okay. But she immediately knew something was wrong. Besides, my mom had already told her that she was worried. "Sis, what's wrong?" she asked.

I wouldn't answer her. As much as I wanted to, I couldn't tell her. After a while she said, "Sis, I already know. You can tell me. It's not going to change anything. I love you." I just cried into the phone. I'm not sure I ever admitted the truth to her, but she kept talking. She let me know that she didn't care who I loved or was in a relationship with; it didn't change her feelings for me. She would never disown or be embarrassed by me. She promised she would also never allow anyone else to disrespect me. The love she shared through that phone call changed everything. At the very least I had hope, and at the most I had someone who would stand by me and fight with and for me. I had an ally.

She was as good as her word. She listened. Even when I dated people who were far from Ms. Right, she defended and supported my right to date them, and when we talked about these relationships, it was always within the context of the person, not their gender. She validated. She would tell people, "If you have a problem with my sister, you have a problem with me." And she raised my niece and nephew to be the same way. She fought the battles and took on the tough conversations with our mom and others who, once they knew, were having a hard time understanding or accepting my choices.

My mom went through her process as well and is now someone I go to regularly to discuss relationship stuff, but my sister was there from the beginning. Having just one person that I knew would love me no matter what gave me indescribable strength. I lost some friends—I use that word loosely—but knowing I could never lose my sister was empowering. Allyship changes lives. Your kindness, your smile, your acceptance, your ability to open up and talk to another person could be all the kindness that someone receives in a day, but it can make all the difference.

WHITE MEN, GET IN THE GAME

We have to understand that we are here to uplift and support each other. That's the best way to rise above our BS. We can do it quietly, one person at a time. Sometimes we have to get loud and fight. Protests, demonstrations, petitions, are all great for building morale and momentum. But often the most effective action you can take is simply looking around and figuring out where you can use your power for good by reaching out a hand or making opportunities available to people who are often left out. As important as it is to take to the streets in protest of injustice, we must also make noise in our companies. White leaders, this is where you come in: companies can execute change that positively affects your employees' quality of life with the stroke of a pen. There's never a need to wait for litigation, which can take years, to do the right thing. For instance, in 2020 the U.S. Supreme Court finally ruled that the 1964 Civil Rights Act protects gay, lesbian, and transgender employees from discrimination based upon race. Litigation started in 2014. But no one with company decision-making power had to wait all that time to act. Many companies already had antidiscrimination, anti-harassment, LGBTQ+ inclusive policies on their books, even before the Supreme Court ruling.

Who has the most power? White men. It's just true. You hold the majority of our legislative seats. You are the decision makers at most media and entertainment companies, as well as sports franchises. Despite women consistently outnumbering men on college campuses, men make up over half of the college presidents in the country, and 68.5 percent of them are white.[5] Finally, while women have made enormous strides in claiming executive leadership over the last decade, only 7.4 percent are at the head of the nation's Fortune 500 companies,[6] with less than 2 percent of those women of color.[7] As of March 2022, there are two Black female CEOs of a Fortune 500 company.[8] Where women do hold executive power, over 65 percent are concentrated in HR, DEI, and Legal.[9] Men hold the majority of the executive and managerial positions. White men can move mountains to support BIPOC, women, LGBTQ+, and other marginalized communities, and rarely worry about how it will affect your upward climb.

Noise makers don't always have power, but when they look like the people in power, they can often make themselves heard. Powerful people, on the other hand, don't always have to make noise to implement change. They can just take it upon themselves to act. Steve Turnbo was one of those powerful people.

For many years, I owned the only diversity communications firm in the state of Oklahoma. It was basically a public relations and marketing firm geared toward helping clients reach diverse markets. I may have been the only one in the state even focused on diversity and inclusion during those early years. I didn't know of anyone else talking about it, and I'm certain no one else had created a business around the concept in Oklahoma. It was the main reason for my struggle. I was selling something no one thought they needed. Early in my career, in order to make a case for its importance, I did some research and then put together a presentation to show PR and advertising firms how much buying power they were missing out on by ignoring the number of Asian, Hispanic, Black, and Native American consumers that lived in our state, buying power they could reach if they diversified their advertising and marketing. I had data that showed how large, white-owned firms in cities like Chicago, Houston, and DC were buying partnerships into the small Black-owned, Hispanic-owned, and LGBTQ+-owned firms to access those markets, and were seeing increased profits. People met with me, but almost none had any interest in pursuing these markets. One even asked me why I thought anyone would possibly care about this. Black-owned businesses and even the publisher of *Black Enterprise* magazine applauded my vision, then encouraged me to move out of the state. I would get nowhere in Oklahoma, they told me. But I had to stay in my home state because no one was doing this work here, whereas I would have been one of many in another state, and Oklahoma needed to become aware of diversified markets.

Then I met Steve, a partner at one of the oldest PR firms in the state. In his perennial bow tie and sweater vest, he looked like the last person who would feel compelled to help break down BS. But after listening to what I had to say, he agreed that diversifying was something that needed to happen in Tulsa. He wasn't sure he could convince his two partners to bring me in, but he gave me a chance to present to them and his entire staff. It didn't go well. As soon as I entered the room, I could feel I was getting no love except from Steve. The vibe and facial expression from one woman were so put-out and irritated I turned into a stuttering mess. Of course, the partners turned me down. But Steve wasn't done with me yet. We stayed in touch. He continued to validate my efforts, listening when I'd tell him about the latest rude comment or mean behavior that had been lobbed at me, and insisting I ignore those people and keep doing what I was doing. "You're on to something," he'd say. "I'm starving!" I'd reply. "Keep going," he'd reassure me. "It's going to take a while." He would tell me that all the time—it's going to take a while. But he was absolutely positive that one day, companies would recognize that what I was saying was true and that they were going to miss out on something huge if they didn't act soon. No matter how much rejection I faced, every time I'd talk to Steve, he'd listen and validate, and I knew I would live to fight another day.

And he acted. Any time he could bring me in on a project, he did. He threw me business every year. He was a board member for the Tulsa Regional Chamber, and when a spot opened up, he recommended me. Once I was there, he encouraged me to speak up. Every time we had to discuss anything related to North Tulsa, which was the Black side of town, or anything else that would primarily affect the Black community, he'd ask me what I thought. He encouraged me to speak on all issues, but felt that any issues or decisions regarding diverse people or communities should certainly have my input. When I had ideas, I'd run them by him, or show him my proposals, and he'd give me his expert opinion. When the national PR conference took place in San Francisco, I had barely two dimes to rub together. I spent almost everything I had just to make the trip, so I had nothing left to spend on joining groups in the evening for entertainment. But Steve was my ally. When he found out I was at the conference, he made sure a place for me was reserved at every table and that I had entrance to every meeting at the conference that interested me. Steve didn't do this out of charity. I was working my ass off. I'd proven myself to him; he was just making sure that a person with few connections or advantages was visible to the industry she wanted to help. He was the embodiment of allyship, a man in a position of power and decision-making who used his power to pull me up the ladder.

WHITE WOMEN, WE NEED YOU TOO!

The woman who scowled at me during my presentation for Steve Turnbo's PR firm? Eventually she left to work for another company. A few years later, with the Oklahoma governor's support, I launched an initiative called X Out Exclusion, which pitched diversity as a stimulant for economic growth. The governor threw a private fundraising dinner at his house, and this woman was invited. This time when I pitched her, though, she didn't dismiss me. This time she was able to see my vision, and she donated $20,000. A decade later, we served together in a leadership program and became friends. Today, she's one of my biggest fans, sharing my social media posts, offering me advice when I ask for it. She became an ally. White women have their own hills to climb in a world built by and for men, but they still have more power than women of color and trans women.

AVOID TOKENISM

When you're pulling BIPOC or other people not part of the majority into your circle and making sure they're acknowledged and recognized for their work, make sure you're not only doing that when it makes you or the company look good. If you decide to implement a DEI program, you better not expect the few BIPOC teammates at your company to advise you on it or run it. When I was involved in the Tulsa Regional Chamber of Commerce, I received a phone call every damn time a photo shoot was scheduled. I became good friends with the PR person in charge of these photo shoots and finally asked her if the reason I was called each time was because I was the only Black person she knew. She laughed. Her answer was, well, sorta. She knew other Black people, but I was heavily involved and on the leadership team for Tulsa's Young Professionals, which was one of the fastest-growing young professional groups in the U.S. during that time. The chamber was the TYPros sponsor, and I was also on the chamber board. She also knew it was vitally important that the chamber of commerce signal to the city that it was interested in promoting diversity and inclusion. A website dominated by pictures of white people wouldn't do that. I told her she should have led with that.

Transparency is key. When you let people in on your thinking so they understand that you are coming from a good place, they're always more inclined to help you see your ideas through. People should be recognized and selected for jobs and positions based on the quality of their work, absolutely. But sometimes you need expertise, or a perspective grounded in lived experience, someone who can tell you when you're about to make a huge mistake and when you're on track. If you're bringing in someone LGBTQ+ to improve your outreach to that population, or someone Latino because you want to build closer ties to the Hispanic community, just say so! If they don't want to do it, they won't do it. Besides, it's BS to assume that every Latino is connected to or invested in the Hispanic community. Cast your net wide enough, and you might find a white person who grew up in a Hispanic community, speaks perfect Spanish, and understands that populations' needs. Being inclusive isn't about finding representation for representation's sake—it's about opening up opportunities to a broader variety of people and allowing them to shine. We have to resist our natural inclination to turn toward people who remind us of us. That tendency is one of the reasons the tech industry is so blindingly white, male, and rife with a reputation for dude-bro-ism, and why BIPOC entrepreneurs have such a hard time finding investors. I have to admit that I'm also sometimes guilty of this for a different reason. I want to give a hand up to all my Black sistas out there trying to live out their entrepreneurial dreams. I want to hire them to show how powerful we are together. I feel justified because of everything you've read in this book. Who else is going to give "us" a chance, if not "us" when we have the ability to do so? However, I'm very aware of this instinct, and while it remains important to me, I still make space for people not like me because I truly believe that diversity makes business stronger and better.

My speaking manager, Shannyn, is a white woman I met over the phone in 2016. She was doing some behind-the-scenes work for a bureau that I reached out to for representation, even though I worried they wouldn't prioritize me because they had so many speakers. As she gave me speaking industry advice and tips, we became friends. One day Shannyn informed me that she had finished her assignment and would be fully focusing on her speaker management business, where she already managed two other clients. I jumped at the opportunity to ask her if she would represent me, thinking that with her, I might be a bigger fish in a smaller pond. And yet, I was nervous. Not only did she live in Canada, but she was also white, and despite all my efforts, my distrust of white people still lingered quietly in the back of my mind. How could I be sure that she wouldn't just take my money and do nothing for me? I didn't have a dime to spare.

In the end, hiring Shannyn was one of the best business decisions I ever made. Together, we have built an incredible speaking business while working with some of the top companies in the world.

RADICAL ACT

Be better than your BS by intentionally creating inclusive environments, even when it makes you uncomfortable, and reap the rewards both socially and financially.

If you're transparent, many people will be happy to help you with your mission to diversify even if they know they will serve as the poster child for a while. Once I understood the purpose of the photographs I was asked to pose for, I felt comfortable participating. If I hadn't thought the chamber was truly trying to create change, I wouldn't have been involved. What pisses people off is when they realize they're being used as a prop while no real effort or investment is being put into moving the needle for the cause. Do that, and you'll be worse off than if you'd never tried to change things in the first place. Word gets around.

DON'T PLAY WHITE SAVIOR

There was a time around 2015 and 2016, as the number of Black men, women, and children killed by police officers gained increasing media attention, that Black Lives Matter chapter meetings swelled with first-time white visitors.

A friend shared with me something that happened at one particularly crowded and emotional event. After the names of the dead had been called and the leaders read over the minutes from the last meeting, the organizer at the dais asked if anyone needed to speak. A white woman raised her hand. She stood up holding a piece of paper in her hand, and said that she'd made a list of business contacts and resources she thought perhaps the chapter ought to try contacting for support. She'd barely gotten the words out before the room erupted with cries for her to sit down and be quiet. Did she really think the group hadn't been reaching out to local businesses in the years before she'd finally decided to come and see what they were about? Did she really believe that in all that time, the reason they hadn't solved the problem of police violence and racism in America was because they hadn't been privy to her infinite knowledge about how to organize and strategize? Was it truly possible she understood the issues better than they did? It was a brutal takedown.

I have no doubt in my mind that this white woman never intended to step on anyone's toes, and that she sincerely meant well. However, she displayed an astounding arrogance, couched in care and concern, in assuming that despite the fact she was a newcomer, not only to this organization but to the entire issue at hand, she had the same authority in this space as every other space she probably operated in. Her actions showed she saw herself the same way many white people new to race-or-social-justice work do—as the group's savior, swooping in to save the day for people that had simply been lost before she showed up to show them the way.

White saviors get so caught up in their vision of the good they want to do, they neglect to center the people and the cause for whom they're doing it. They tend to dominate a situation, but leave no impact on the systems that caused the situation. They make issues about themselves without asking any questions to truly understand the situation. They play at being allies without doing the real work, or taking the risks of actually being one. Ultimately, all they do is get in the way of real progress.

I often think about this woman and wonder if she ever came back to a meeting, or if she continued to try to get involved with anti-racist work in some other way. Was she so hurt and embarrassed by the reception she got that she swore she'd never try again, or did she think long and hard about what had happened, and try to learn from the experience? I hope she recognized that the civil rights or other historic figures she likely admired were treated far worse than that on a regular basis. I hope she decided that if they could stick it out and keep coming back until they saw progress made, she could lick her wounds and try again, perhaps this time with a bit more humility and a commitment to the radical acts of listening and validating before assuming she knew what actions to take.

A true ally offers support without drawing attention to themselves. They use their privilege to empower the work that needs to be done, not to take over the work from people with more experience and better understanding of the issues.

OTHER WAYS TO ALLY

Being an ally can be scary for some people. Not everyone will be as comfortable standing up to their peers as my cousin Pete or Steve Turnbo, whether they do it by including an untraditional choice in a project, or just cutting someone off when they start speaking BS nonsense.

It can be intimidating to speak out when we hear something problematic. I understand. The way to get over that is to practice in safe spaces before putting yourself on the line professionally. Speak up at home and with family and friends you know. Push back when you hear BS. Write a blog or social media posts drawing attention to issues you believe your circle needs to become more aware of. Not everyone will approve or applaud you. Engage in conversations and meet people where they are, but don't back down. Just like when you work out to build physical muscle, you have to practice building up your allyship muscles. That's how you develop the spine of steel that allows you to take your efforts into the workplace and really work for greater change.

Another idea is to take to the digital sphere. Call it out when you see a company saying all the right things on Twitter and Instagram but donating to organizations and groups that promote bigotry, racism, and exclusion.

If you're a leader or decision maker, in addition to setting up a DEI office and program, improving your communication channels is a prime place to show allyship and create comfortable work environments that encourage employees to speak up. Review the suggestions in Chapter 8 about updating communication training and the employee handbook so that it uses gender-neutral and inclusive language, and prominently displaying a diversity tab and Culture Commitment on your website. Create feedback channels for employees. Establish a 1-800 number or e-mail address so they can easily report problems to HR. Anonymous reports are hard to act on, but at least someone in the department can keep track of how many of these kinds of reports come in, and use the volume as evidence that something needs to be done.

We always tell children that it's not just what's on the outside that counts, it's what's on the inside. That appearances aren't everything. The same is true for companies. Slapping a single photo or two of a non-white face on your website or recruitment materials isn't inclusive. Posting rainbow flags on your social media channels while donating to organizations that brand the LGBTQ+ community as deviant isn't just not inclusive, it's hypocritical BS. You don't have to be a saint in order to be an ally, but you do have to clean your own house. Those of us on the receiving end of BS need you to. That's why it's so important to work toward Radical Acceptance. It speeds up the pace of change, giving those who care about these things the tools to pitch in and help move things forward to the best of their ability.

CONCLUSION

Not long before I was done with the first draft of this book, I took a flight to Denver. I sat in the window seat, and my chief of content creation, Arielle, was in the middle. Eventually, a white man settled into the aisle seat. Exhausted, I closed my eyes and leaned my head against the side of the plane. I wasn't sleeping, just resting, so I could hear as Arielle and the white man started to chat. He asked what we did and why we were traveling. Arielle informed him that I teach diversity, equity, and inclusion. "So basically, she teaches adults how to respect each other."

"Oh," he replied. "People actually get paid for that?"

The man informed Arielle that for the first time, his company had a Black, female CEO. He then added that working with his new boss marked "the first time I've ever talked to or met an articulate Black woman." Unfortunately, he explained, as articulate as she was, she was incompetent, but there was no way the company board was going to get rid of her. They were too afraid.

Upon hearing this series of microaggressions, I picked my head up. I knew what I was supposed to do. I'm trained for it. I train other people to do it. I opened my mouth to start pointing out to the man everything problematic about what he'd said, but then instead I looked at him and Arielle, shook my head, and said out loud, "Not today." Then I inserted my earbuds and rolled back toward the window with my eyes closed so I could shut out the whole scene.

Arielle continued the conversation, working hard to keep her composure. Feigning ignorance, she asked, "Why would the board be afraid to let someone go if they were clearly not a good fit for the job?"

The man continued with no hint of self-awareness, "Oh, it's because she's Black and they're afraid they'll be accused of racism."

"Interesting," said Arielle. "That makes me curious about the demographics of the board."

"They're white," the man told her, as if this detail should go without saying.

"Right," said Arielle. "You know, your situation supports the case for ensuring more diversity exists at all levels within a company, doesn't it? It's harder to accuse a group of racism when it's comprised of people from all races and backgrounds, wouldn't you say?"

She told me later that she was ready to spend the whole plane ride working to move the needle and getting this man to acknowledge his biases, but shortly after their exchange started, he was moved to a different seat, and Arielle got to relax and enjoy some shows on her iPad instead.

It can take energy and effort to stay in Radical Acceptance mode, and sometimes we're tired and need to take a break. Even me. I'll admit, as optimistic as I am when I see the real effort companies are putting in to make the workplace more equitable, there are days where it feels like the more steps we take forward, the more we take back. You've surely noticed by now that the only reason the Radical Acts I propose throughout this book might be considered radical is that not many people dare to do them. In fact, at this point just reading this book is a Radical Act. It's my sincerest hope that one day these gestures and actions will be so commonplace and second nature, they won't be worth mentioning. We're not even close. I keep thinking that one day I'm going to stop hearing and encountering the same biases over and over, but they keep coming. They may sound a little different than in the past, they may be couched in slightly different terms, but many of the biases people carry are as prevalent today as they were 50 years ago. Our grandparents were wrestling with this stuff. Will we ever move past it? Does the fact that it's taking us so long to fix our BS mean what I'm trying to do is impossible?

Then I get reminders that it's not. For example, when a white woman approaches me after a talk to tell me that she arrived with a closed mind but is leaving with an open one. Or when following a keynote, a Black woman thanks me for putting her struggles into easily digestible terms because for the first time, she thinks the white folks around her finally get what she's been trying to tell them for years. Or when a man tells me the most important thing he learned from me is that we have to be kind to each other. (Mind you, this man was at least in his 60s!) There was also the white man who came up to me in tears to tell me how badly his company needed to hear my message, even if they didn't want to, and that if I ever needed him for anything, he would be there. Those are the moments that make up for the difficult moments like the one Arielle and I sat through on the airplane.

If I can get just one person to change their perspective, to attempt Radical Acceptance, to aim to become better than their BS, all the effort is worth it. That one person is going to carry my message much further than I can on my own. That one person just might reach two people who've never heard of me. And maybe they'll reach two more. I work on the micro level, but I know that if we can affect enough people on the micro level, we'll change the macro level. It does take effort, but as the old saying goes, many hands make light work.

That doesn't mean the work will always be easy. At the end of one of my trainings, a woman whose child had recently begun to transition from male to female began to cry. "My son has been struggling with this his entire life, but I only found out about it two weeks ago, and suddenly I'm supposed to remember his new name and use the right pronoun every time. I love my child whoever they want to be, but he's angry that I can't just turn on a dime and adapt perfectly after knowing him as a boy for the first twenty years of our life together. I'm supportive, but I have to be able to ask questions, and I have to be able to make mistakes without feeling like I'm going to lose him."

I believe this dynamic is being played out across the nation. While Black folks, POC, and many of the LGBTQ+ community have been having these conversations since they could talk, many people, especially straight white folks, are new to the discussion. If that's you, it's great that you're willing to listen, learn, and add your voice. But only so long as you act at the same time. Because talk alone is cheap and empty. Keep asking yourself questions as you go through your day, or as you manage a meeting, or as you conduct a Zoom call: How can I create trust and comfort? How can I be sure I'm being a good ally? How can I fix my communication strategies so that I deliver a message in a way it can be received? How can I make sure diversity is reflected in my employees, vendors, contractors? How can I make sure the board looks like the community we serve? You won't always get things right, or at least, you won't always make the progress you hoped you'd make as quickly as you'd like. Stick with it. We all need to give each other grace. We must give people a chance to show us their hearts. This is an evolution. Radical Acceptance is a transformative process with a vast potential to create the change we want to see. It doesn't only work if you work for a corporation. Radical Acceptance can be used if you sit on a nonprofit board, work with a group for a community-based project, if you are managing your family, or just need to assess some things personally.

I won't lie. If you do the inner work to be better than your BS, you may change more than your BS. You may change your whole life. You might lose friends, loved ones, or a faith community. Because not everyone will approve. But achieving Radical Acceptance is worth it. As author Iyanla Vanzant says, you've got to be willing to lose everything to gain yourself. You also have to be brave enough to be wrong to get your company culture right. And we have to love enough to stop judging each other in the moment so we can win humanity in the end.

BREAK DOWN YOUR BS RESOURCES

No culture is a monolith, and it would be impossible to include a representative of every perspective that deserves attention, but here are some books, podcasts, websites, and other resources that feature diverse points of view.

MOVIES

    12 Years a Slave
    Battle of the Sexes
    Black Panther
    Bros
    Carol
    Coco
    Crazy Rich Asians
    Disclosure
    Do the Right Thing
    Get Out
    Hidden Figures
    Love, Simon
    Milk
    Minari
    Miss Representation
    Moana

Moonlight
Paris Is Burning
Princess and the Frog
Queen and Slim
The 13th
The Big Sick
The Mask You Live In
When They See Us
Zootopia

BOOKS

Agewise by Margaret Morganroth Gullette
All American Boys by Jason Reynolds and Brian Kiely
Allyship in Action by Julie Kratz
America and the Challenges of Religious Diversity by Robert Wuthnow
American Born Chinese by Gene Yang
The Anti-Racism Journal by Faith Brooks
Better Allies by Karen Caitlin and Sally McGraw
Citizen Illegal by José Olivarez
A Disability History of the United States by Kim E. Nielsen
How to Be an Antiracist by Ibram X. Kendi
I'm Still Here by Austin Channing Brown
The New Jim Crow by Michelle Alexander
Queer by Meg-John Barker
Toxic Inequality by Thomas Shapiro
White Fragility by Robin Di Angelo
Why Are All the Black Kids Sitting Together at the Cafeteria Table? by Beverly Daniel Tatum, Ph.D.

TV SHOWS

A Different World

Atypcial

Awkwafina Is Nora from Queens

Black-ish

Insecure

L Word

Master of None

Ms. Marvel

Never Have I Ever

One Day at a Time

Pachinko

Party of Five (2020 Remake)

Pose

Special

Star Trek: The Next Generation

The Healing Powers of Dude

Uncoupled

Work in Progress

PODCASTS

Allyship is a Verb

Codeswitch

Culture Happens

Identity Politics

Latinos Who Lunch

Leading with Empathy and Allyship

Making Gay History, the Podcast

The Power of Privilege and Allyship

Queer America

Teaching Hard History

The Will to Change

Women at Work

WEBSITES

The Black Wall Street Times,
www.theblackwallsttimes.com

Guide to Allyship, www.guidetoallyship.com

Indigenous Cultures Institute
(www.indigenouscultures.org/)

Osiyo TV, www.osiyo.tv

The Righteous Among the Nations, www.yadvashem
.org/righteous/stories.html

Stanford Graduate School of Business Anti-Racism
and Allyship 7-Day Journey, http://www.gsb
-sites.stanford.edu/anti-racism-and-allyship

SOCIAL MEDIA

@AsianBossGirl

Brené Brown @BreneBrown

Conscious Lee @theconsciouslee

Diversity, Inclusion, Equity, Justice, Belonging &
Liberation (Facebook)

@everydaymiddleeast

Franchesca "Chescaleigh" Ramsey, MTV Decoded,
@chescaleigh

Faiza Rammuny, @expirednfabulous

Hispanic Community (Facebook)

Julie Kratz, Next Pivot Point, @nextpivotpoint

LGBT Advocate (Facebook)

Lift Black Voices (Facebook)

Native American Blood (Facebook)

@NextShark

USA LGBT Pride (Facebook)

White Allies for Black Lives Coalition (Facebook)

#whiteallies (Facebook and LinkedIn)

ENDNOTES

Introduction

1. "Oklahoma Quick Facts," United States Census Bureau, https://www.census.gov/quickfacts/fact/table/OK/RHI125219.

2. Josh Trujillo, "Beyond May 29: Lessons from Starbucks Anti-Bias Training—and What's Next," Starbucks.com, July 2, 2018, https://stories.starbucks.com/stories/2018/beyond-may-29-lessons-from-starbucks-anti-bias-training-and-whats-next/.

3. Patrick Murray, "National: Protesters' Anger Justified Even if Actions May Not Be," Monmouth University Poll, June 2, 2020, https://www.monmouth.edu/polling-institute/documents/monmouthpoll_us_060220.pdf/.

4. Bowdeya Tweh, "Corporate Executives Are Pressed to Improve Racial Equity in Workplaces," *The Wall Street Journal*, June 11, 2020, https://www.wsj.com/livecoverage/protests-george-floyd-death-2020-06-11/card/4qIrbPgOK7E1sP1ctgnw.

5. Kim Parker and Ruth Igielnik, "On the Cusp of Adulthood and Facing an Uncertain Future: What We Know About Gen Z So Far," Pew Research Center, May 14, 2020, https://www.pewresearch.org/social-trends/2020/05/14/on-the-cusp-of-adulthood-and-facing-an-uncertain-future-what-we-know-about-gen-z-so-far-2/.

6. Jeffrey M. Jones, "LGBT Identification Rises to 5.6% in Latest U.S. Estimate," Gallup, February 24, 2021, https://news.gallup.com/poll/329708/lgbt-identification-rises-latest-estimate.aspx.

7. "Deloitte Global Millennial Survey 2020," Deloitte, https://www2.deloitte.com/global/en/pages/about-deloitte/articles/millennialsurvey.html.

8. Hunt, et al., "Why Diversity Matters," McKinsey & Co, January 1, 2015, https://www.mckinsey.com/business-functions/organization/our-insights/why-diversity-matters.

9. Lorenzo, et al., "How Diverse Teams Boost Innovation," Boston Consulting Group, January 23, 2018, https://www.bcg.com/en-us/publications/2018/how-diverse-leadership-teams-boost-innovation.aspx.

10. Josh Bersin, "Why Diversity and Inclusion Has Become a Business Priority," March 16, 2019, http://joshbersin.com/2015/12/why-diversity-and-inclusion-will-be-a-top-priority-for-2016/.

11. Zweig, et al., "Toxic Culture Is Driving the Great Resignation," MITSloan Management Review, https://sloanreview.mit.edu/article/toxic-culture-is-driving-the-great-resignation/.

Chapter 1

1. Pippa Stevens, "Companies Are Making Bold Promises About Greater Diversity, but There's a Long Way to Go," CNBC, https://www.cnbc.com/2020/06/11/companies-are-making-bold-promises-about-greater-diversity-theres-a-long-way-to-go.html.

2. James Norman, "A VC's Guide to Investing in Black Founders," Harvard Business Review, June 19, 2020, https://hbr.org/2020/06/a-vcs-guide-to-investing-in-Black-founders.

3. Sarab Kochhar and Institute for Public Relations: "Nearly Half of American Millennials Say a Diverse and Inclusive Workplace Is an Important Factor in a Job Search," December 4, 2017, Institute for PR, https://instituteforpr.org/nearly-half-american-millennials-say-diverse-inclusive-workplace-important-factor-job-search/.

4. Dayana Yochim, "Pride Month: 12 Key Numbers Highlighting the Economic Status, Challenges that LGBTQ People Face," MSNBC, June 22, 2020, https://www.nbcnews.com/know-your-value/feature/pride-month-12-key-numbers-highlighting-economic-status-challenges-lgbtq-ncna1231820.

5. "GlassDoor Survey Finds Three in Five U.S. Employees Have Experienced or Witnessed Discrimination Based on Age, Race, Gender or LGBTQ Identity at Work," Glassdoor, October 23, 2019, https://www.glassdoor.com/blog/app/uploads/sites/2/LGBTQ_survey_final-2.pdf.

6. Joy Collective, "The Crown Research Study," Dove, 2019, https://static1.squarespace.com/static/5edc69fd622c36173f56651f/t/5edea a2fe5ddef345e087361/1591650865168/Dove_research _brochure2020_FINAL3.pdf.

7. Jeffrey C. Miller, "2020 EEOC Statistics—More Money and Fewer Charges," BMD, March 16, 2021, https://www.bmdllc.com/resources/blog/2020-eeoc-statistics-more-money-and-fewer-charges/.

8. Kristin Baver, "Telling the Odds: Anthony Daniels and His Memoir I Am C-3PO," Star Wars, December 12, 2019, https://www.starwars.com/news/anthony-daniels-memoir-interview.

9. Tom Reiman, "32 Nightmarish Movie Costumes Actors Hated Wearing," Collider, June 15, 2019, https://collider.com/galleries/movie-costumes-actors-hated/.

10. "Sidelined, Suffocated, and Nearly Baked Alive: The Story of the Man Who Didn't Want to Play C-3PO," Independent, November 1, 2019, https://www.independent.co.uk/arts-entertainment/films/features/anthony-daniels-star-wars-c3po-memoir-book-inside -story-a9178096.html.

11. El Kharazi, et al., "Retaliation—Making It Personal," U.S. Equal Employment Opportunity Commission, https://www.eeoc.gov/retaliation-making-it-personal.

12. U.S. Equal Employment Opportunity Commission, "EEOC Releases Fiscal Year 2020 Enforcement and Litigation Data," February 26, 2021, Accounted for over half: https://www.eeoc.gov/newsroom/eeoc-releases-fiscal-year-2020-enforcement-and-litigation-data.

Chapter 2

1. James Brooke, "Witnesses Trace Brutal Killing of Gay Student," The New York Times, November 21, 1998.

2. "Authorities Trace Cellphone to Capture Man Accused in Pursuit Across Tulsa Airport," Tulsa World, https://tulsaworld.com/news/local/crime-and-courts/authorities-trace-cellphone-to-capture-man -accused-in-pursuit-across-tulsa-airport-runways-and-fatal/article _ee1f2fc0-2cf6-5b98-9411-0d94c897e930.html.

3. Rosy Cordero, "UCLA's 2021 Hollywood Diversity Report Reveals TV Content from Diverse Writers & with Diverse Casts Resonated with Pandemic Audiences," https://deadline.com/2021/10/ucla-hollywood -diversity-report-tv-representation-inclusion-1234862431/.

4. "'Ms. Marvel' Is the Highest Scoring Disney Plus Marvel Series Ever," *Forbes*, Paul Tassi, https://www.forbes.com/sites/paultassi/2022/06/08/ms-marvel-is-the-highest-scoring-disney-plus-marvel-series-ever/?sh=22f400741d26.

5. Jessica Wolf, "2021 Hollywood Diversity Report: Audiences Showed Up for Diverse Films in Theaters, Online," UCLA, April 22, 2021, https://newsroom.ucla.edu/releases/2021-hollywood-diversity-report.

6. Richard Jean So and Gus Wezerek, "Just How White Is the Publishing Industry?" *The New York Times*, December 11, 2020, https://www.nytimes.com/interactive/2020/12/11/opinion/culture/diversity-publishing-industry.html.

7. Robertson, et al., "Race and Leadership in the News Media 2021: Evidence from Five Markets," Reuters Institute, https://reutersinstitute.politics.ox.ac.uk/race-and-leadership-news-media-2021-evidence-five-markets.

8. Beth Daley, "How Young Children Can Develop Racial Bias—and What that Means," *The Conversation*, March 20, 2018, https://theconversation.com/how-young-children-can-develop-racial-biases-and-what-that-means-93150.

9. Pirchio, et al., "A Chip Off the Old Block: Parents' Subtle Ethnic Prejudice Predicts Children's Implicit Prejudice," *Sec. Developmental Psychology*, February 9, 2018, https://www.frontiersin.org/articles/10.3389/fpsyg.2018.00110/full.

10. Richard Jean So and Gus Wezerek, "Just How White Is the Publishing Industry?" *The New York Times*, December 11, 2020, https://www.nytimes.com/interactive/2020/12/11/opinion/culture/diversity-publishing-industry.html.

11. "#PublishingPaidMe and a Day of Action Reveal an Industry Reckoning," *The New York Times*, June 10, 2020, https://www.nytimes.com/2020/06/08/books/publishingpaidme-publishing-day-of-action.html.

Chapter 3

1. Richie Zweigenhaft, "Fortune 500 CEOs, 2000–2020: Still Male, Still White," *The Society Pages*, October 28, 2020, https://thesocietypages.org/specials/fortune-500-ceos-2000-2020-still-male-still-white/.

2. Halla Tómasdóttir, "The Inclusion Revolution in Leadership: Changing Who Leads Will Transform How We Do Business," *Fortune*, April 28, 2021, https://fortune.com/2021/04/28/leadership-inclusion-revolution-c-suite-boardroom-diversity/.

3. Cydney Posner, "New Survey: Diversity on Fortune 100 and Fortune 500 Boards," Cooley PubCo, June 9, 2021, https://cooleypubco.com/2021/06/09/board-diversity-fortune-500/.

4. Cydney Posner, "New Survey: Diversity on Fortune 100 and Fortune 500 Boards," Cooley PubCo, June 9, 2021, https://cooleypubco.com/2021/06/09/board-diversity-fortune-500/.

5. Cydney Posner, "New Survey: Diversity on Fortune 100 and Fortune 500 Boards," Cooley PubCo, June 9, 2021, https://cooleypubco.com/2021/06/09/board-diversity-fortune-500/.

6. Huang, et al., "Women in the Workplace 2019," McKinsey & Company, October 2019, https://www.mckinsey.com/~/media/McKinsey/Featured%20Insights/Gender%20Equality/Women%20in%20the%20Workplace%202019/Women-in-the-workplace-2019.ashx.

7. Huang, et al., "Women in the Workplace 2019," McKinsey & Company, October 2019, https://www.mckinsey.com/~/media/McKinsey/Featured%20Insights/Gender%20Equality/Women%20in%20the%20Workplace%202019/Women-in-the-workplace-2019.ashx.

8. Michael Martin, "Scholarships: Who Gets Them and Why?" NPR, March 17, 2011, https://www.npr.org/templates/story/story.php?storyId=134623124.

9. https://outleadership.com/insights/fair-representation-better-outcomes/

10. Maria Aspan, "Fortune 500 CEOs Praise Landmark LGBTQ Antidiscrimination Ruling," *Fortune*, June 16, 2020, https://fortune.com/2020/06/16/fortune-500-ceos-supreme-court-lgbtq-ruling/.

11. Lauren A. Rivera, "Hiring as Cultural Matching: The Case of Elite Professional Service Firms," *American Sociological Review*, 2012, https://www.asanet.org/sites/default/files/savvy/journals/ASR/Dec12ASRFeature.pdf; https://www.hbs.edu/recruiting/insights-and-advice/blog/post/actively-addressing-unconscious-bias-in-recruiting.

12. Rebecca Perron, "Age Discrimination Continues to Hold Older Workers Back," AARP Research, May 2021, https://www.aarp.org/research/topics/economics/info-2021/older-workers-new-skills-covid-19-pandemic.htmlDEI.

13. Phyllis Weiss Haserot, "How Organizations Can Address Ageism as Part of Their DEI Strategy," *Thomson Reuters*, September 14, 2021, https://www.thomsonreuters.com/en-us/posts/legal/addressing-ageism/.

14. Jensen, et al., "The Chance That Two People Chosen at Random Are of Different Race or Ethnicity Groups Has Increased Since 2010," United States Census, August 12, 2021, https://www.census

.gov/library/stories/2021/08/2020-united-states-population-more
-racially-ethnically-diverse-than-2010.html.

15. "Census Data Shows Widening Diversity," *The Washington Post*, https://www.washingtonpost.com/dc-md-va/2021/08/12/census-data-race-ethnicity-neighborhoods/.

16. John Della Volpe, *Fight: How Gen Z Is Channeling Their fear and Passion to Save America*, (New York: St. Martin's Press, 2021), 13.

Chapter 4

1. Generation Alpha, or the Divergents: Caroline Bologna, "What's the Deal With Generation Alpha?" HuffPost, Nobember 8, 2019, updated September 25, 2021, https://www.huffpost.com/entry/generation-alpha-after-gen-z_l_5d420ef4e4b0aca341181574#:~:text=In%202005%2C%20social%20researcher%20Mark,years%20back%20a%20bit%20later.

2. A. H. Maslow, "A Theory of Human Motivation," *Classics in the History of Psychology*, 1943, http://psychclassics.yorku.ca/Maslow/motivation.htm.

3. Roy F. Baumeister and Mark R. Leary, "The Need to Belong: The Desire for Interpersonal Attachments as a Fundamental Human Motivation," *Psychological Bulletin* 117, no. 3, (1995): 497–529. http://persweb.wabash.edu/facstaff/hortonr/articles%20for%20class/baumeister%20and%20leary.pdf.

4. Dr. Matthew Lieberman and Dr. Naomi Eisenberger, "The Pains and Pleasures of Social Life: A Social Cognitive Neuroscience Approach," *NeuroLeadership Journal* (2008).

5. Amy Patterson Neubert, "Professor: Pain of Ostracism Can Be Deep, Long-Lasting," Purdue University, May 10, 2011, https://www.purdue.edu/newsroom/research/2011/110510WilliamsOstracism.html.

6. Amy Patterson Neubert, "Professor: Pain of Ostracism Can Be Deep, Long-Lasting," Purdue University, May 10, 2011, https://www.purdue.edu/newsroom/research/2011/110510WilliamsOstracism.html.

7. Amy Patterson Neubert, "Professor: Pain of Ostracism Can Be Deep, Long-Lasting," Purdue University, May 10, 2011, https://www.purdue.edu/newsroom/research/2011/110510WilliamsOstracism.html.

8. Patricia Faison Hewlin, "And the Award for Best Actor Goes to . . . Facades of Conformity in Organizational Settings," *Academy of Management Review* 28, No. 4 (2003): 633–642.

9. Amy Patterson Neubert, "Professor: Pain of Ostracism Can Be Deep, Long-Lasting," Purdue University, May 10, 2011, https://www.purdue .edu/newsroom/research/2011/110510WilliamsOstracism.html.

10. American Psychological Association, https://www.apa.org/monitor/ julaug04/standing; https://www.exeter.ac.uk/news/featurednews/ title_500331_en.html.

11. Dr. Matthew Lieberman and Dr. Naomi Eisenberger, "The Pains and Pleasures of Social Life: A Social Cognitive Neuroscience Approach," *NeuroLeadership Journal* (2008).

12. Dr. Matthew Lieberman and Dr. Naomi Eisenberger, "The Pains and Pleasures of Social Life: A Social Cognitive Neuroscience Approach," *NeuroLeadership Journal* (2008): 5.

Chapter 5

1. Karen Weise, "Amazon Workers Urge Bezos to Match His Words on Race With Actions," *The New York Times*, June 24, 2020, https:// www.nytimes.com/2020/06/24/technology/amazon-racial -inequality.html.

2. Joe Berkowitz, "The Internet Noticed What's Wrong with the NFL's Anti-Racism Super Bowl Ad," *Fast Company*, https://www .fastcompany.com/90602465/the-internet-noticed-whats-wrong -with-the-nfls-anti-racism-super-bowl-ad.

3. Sally Ho, "'Empty Words': Companies Touting Black Lives Matter Accused of Hypocrisy," *Komo News*, June 11, 20202, https:// komonews.com/news/local/empty-words-companies-touting -black-lives-matter-accused-of.

4. Tarpley Hitt, "These Companies Have the Most Hypocritical Black Lives Matter Messaging," *Daily Beast*, https://www.thedailybeast .com/the-companies-with-the-most-hypocritical-black-lives-matter -messaging-from-fox-to-facebook.

5. "NFL's First Black Coach Fritz Pollard Hired in 1921: 'It's Ironic. Not Much Changed,'" *IndyStar*, February 10, 2022, https://www .indystar.com/story/sports/nfl/2022/02/10/first-black-nfl-coach -fritz-pollard-akron-pros/6637386001/.

Chapter 7

1. Neda Ulaby, "Why People Are Rethinking the Words 'Crazy' and 'Insane,'" NPR, July 8, 2019, https://www.npr.org/2019/07/08/739643765/why-people-are-arguing-to-stop-using-the-words-crazy-and-insane.

Chapter 8

1. Shrider, et al., "Income and Poverty in the United States," United States Census Bureau, September 14, 2021, https://www.census.gov/library/publications/2021/demo/p60-273.html.

2. Ana Lankes, "One of the World's First Bans on Gender-Neutral Language," *The New York Times*, https://www.nytimes.com/2022/07/20/world/americas/argentina-gender-neutral-spanish.html.

3. Hannah Devlin, "Unconscious Bias: What Is It and Can It Be Eliminated?" *Psychology*, December 2, 2018, https://www.theguardian.com/uk-news/2018/dec/02/unconscious-bias-what-is-it-and-can-it-be-eliminated.

Chapter 9

1. Archiebald Browne, "Oklahoma's Historic All-Black Towns: Built on Hope, Survived by Pride," NonDoc, July 25, 2019, https://nondoc.com/2019/07/25/oklahoma-historic-all-black-towns/.

2. Amy Harmon and Sabrina Tavernise, "One Big Difference About George Floyd Protests: Many White Faces," *The New York Times*, June 17, 2020, https://www.nytimes.com/2020/06/12/us/george-floyd-white-protesters.html.

3. Buchanan, et al., "Black Lives Matter May Be the Largest Movement in History," *The New York Times*, July 3, 2020, https://www.nytimes.com/interactive/2020/07/03/us/george-floyd-protests-crowd-size.html.

4. "Embracing the 'We,'" Mary Fisher, April 1, 2022, https://www.maryfisher.com/mayijustsaybymaryfisher/embracing-the-we.

5. "College President Demographics and Statistics in the US," Zippia, https://www.zippia.com/college-president-jobs/demographics/.

6. Daniel Kurt, "Corporate Leadership by Gender," Investopedia, updated February 22, 2022, https://www.investopedia.com/corporate-leadership-by-gender-5113708.

7.   Derek Major, "Ursula Burns, the First Black Female Fortune 500 CEO Says 'Being in the Minority Can Be a Career Advantage,'" *Black Enterprise*, March 15, 2022, https://www.blackenterprise.com/ursula-burns-the-first-black-female-fortune-500-ceo-says-being-in-the-minority-can-be-a-career-advantage/.

8.   Derek Major, "Ursula Burns, the First Black Female Fortune 500 CEO Says 'Being in the Minority Can Be a Career Advantage,'" *Black Enterprise*, March 15, 2022, https://www.blackenterprise.com/ursula-burns-the-first-black-female-fortune-500-ceo-says-being-in-the-minority-can-be-a-career-advantage/.

9.   Alex Nesbitt, "Holding White Male Executives Accountable for Diversity and Inclusion," HighPoint Associates, https://www.highpoint-associates.com/2021/03/holding_white_male_executives_accountable_diversity_inclusion/.

INDEX

ACKNOWLEDGMENTS

Thank-yous are not enough for the people mentioned below so I hope you can feel my heart.

Michael Palgon, you are the best agent ever! You kept saying to me, "Think bigger!" I kept thinking, *what the hell. . . I AM thinking big!* It was maddening but here we are. You did everything you said you would do. It made me better and along the way, we became friends. Thank you.

Carolyn Monaco, you were the first person to speak to me when I exited the stage in Vancouver, British Columbia. You said I needed a book. I said I had one. You said I needed a bigger one with a much larger reach because more people needed to hear what I had to say. You found me an agent. Mama Monaco, you never stopped answering my calls or my e-mails. You have become a part of my success. Thank you.

Stephanie Land, you are the GOAT! Thank you for collaborating with me on this book. Your insight and the way you pull my words together are nothing short of amazing. I have learned so much from you and this process. I've also appreciated getting to know you as a friend. Okay, let's get ready for the next one. LOL.

Arielle Davis, I brought you on to be my right hand. Part of your job was to be a thought partner on content and help with the research for this book. It became so much more. You became my confidante, my friend, my partner in life. You went above and beyond what you were paid to do and became my cheerleader, the person who nudged me to keep going when I was frustrated or wanted to give up. You kept reminding me of my "why." You pushed me with your damn questions to dig deeper when I was content that I was finished. I'm forever grateful. I love you.

To anyone who bought or read my first book, attended a speech or workshop, has engaged with me on social media, encouraged me, prayed for me, or sent positive energy my way . . . thank you. I love you for taking the time to let me know that this work is needed. Please continue to be better than your BS.

ABOUT THE AUTHOR

Risha Grant is diversity personified: CEO. Entrepreneur. Black. Female. Small-town born and raised. Bisexual. Spiritual. Ex-preacher's wife. Cusser. Left-handed. Former Division 1 athlete. But these traits alone aren't what make her one of the most powerful and effective DEI experts in the U.S. Hailed as a "cultural competency genius" and renowned for her storytelling chops, humor, and frank delivery, she has made a career of leading her audiences as well as executives and their teams, politicians, civic leaders, and academic directors around the world to Radical Acceptance through a unique bias-busting process of self-examination and concrete advice on how to behave, lead, and manage businesses more inclusively.

In her role as a speaker and multimillion-dollar business owner, Risha has shifted the hearts and minds of her audiences and clients from around the world, including Google, Levi Strauss, Nestlé Purina, Xerox, YouTube, Procter & Gamble, Discover Card Financial Services, Samsung Electronics America, Cox Communications, U.S. Airforce, U.S. Navy, Intuit, NBA's Oklahoma City Thunder, and Harvard University.

She's been featured in various national and international media including *Forbes*, *Entrepreneur* magazine, *Harvard Business Review*, *HR News*, *The Financial Times*, *Glamour Magazine UK*, *Bloomberg Media*, and *Black Enterprise*, among others.

Risha has received numerous honors such as being named one of the: Top 10 Most Powerful Women Leaders in HR, 40 Top Women Keynote Speakers, and Top 100 HR Experts. She was named as 1 in 9 Speakers Turning Crisis into Opportunity by *Entrepreneur* magazine, and for three consecutive years has been an Engagedly Top 100 HR Influencer and Entrepreneur of the Year.

Risha will freely admit that she is a work in progress. She occasionally misuses pronouns. She prejudges others. Sometimes she walks in fear. Yet she has consistently striven to focus on love, and made it her mission to use her passion, persistence, knowledge, and experience to dismantle racism, sexism, classism, and plain old stupidism—including her own. She lives in Tulsa, Oklahoma, with her partner, where when not teaching people how to challenge bias she is busy being the world's best auntie.

To learn more about Risha and her work, visit: www.rishagrant.com.

Hay House Titles of Related Interest

THE SHIFT, the movie,
starring Dr. Wayne W. Dyer
(available as an online streaming video)
www.hayhouse.com/the-shift-movie

***

*BE THE CALM OR BE THE STORM: Leadership Lessons from
a Woman at the Helm,* by Captain Sandy Yawn

*CHANGE ENTHUSIASM: How to Harness the Power of Emotion
for Leadership and Success,* by Cassandra Worthy

*HIGH PERFORMANCE HABITS: How Extraordinary People
Become That Way,* by Brendon Burchard

*KNOW JUSTICE KNOW PEACE: A Transformative Journey
of Social Justice, Anti-Racism, and Healing through the Power
of the Enneagram,* by Deborah Threadgill Egerton, Ph.D.,
with Lisi Mohandessi

*MARKET YOUR GENIUS: How to Generate New Leads,
Get Dream Customers, and Create a Loyal Community,*
by Nikki Nash

All of the above are available at your local bookstore
or may be ordered by visiting:

Hay House USA: www.hayhouse.com®
Hay House Australia: www.hayhouse.com.au
Hay House UK: www.hayhouse.co.uk
Hay House India: www.hayhouse.co.in

All of the above are available at your local bookstore,
or may be ordered by contacting Hay House (see next page).

***

We hope you enjoyed this Hay House book. If you'd like to receive our online catalog featuring additional information on Hay House books and products, or if you'd like to find out more about the Hay Foundation, please contact:

Hay House, Inc., P.O. Box 5100, Carlsbad, CA 92018-5100
(760) 431-7695 or (800) 654-5126
(760) 431-6948 (fax) or (800) 650-5115 (fax)
www.hayhouse.com® • www.hayfoundation.org

———

Published in Australia by: Hay House Australia Pty. Ltd.,
18/36 Ralph St., Alexandria NSW 2015
Phone: 612-9669-4299 • *Fax:* 612-9669-4144
www.hayhouse.com.au

Published in the United Kingdom by: Hay House UK, Ltd.,
The Sixth Floor, Watson House, 54 Baker Street, London W1U 7BU
Phone: +44 (0)20 3927 7290 • *Fax:* +44 (0)20 3927 7291
www.hayhouse.co.uk

Published in India by: Hay House Publishers India,
Muskaan Complex, Plot No. 3, B-2, Vasant Kunj, New Delhi 110 070
Phone: 91-11-4176-1620 • *Fax:* 91-11-4176-1630
www.hayhouse.co.in

———

Access New Knowledge.
Anytime. Anywhere.

Learn and evolve at your own pace
with the world's leading experts.

www.hayhouseU.com

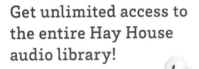

Write Your Book.
Grow Your Business.

AUTHORPRENEUR
MEMBERSHIP BY HAY HOUSE

Discover one of the best ways to **establish** your expertise, strategically **increase** your revenue, organically **attract** more customers, and **deliver** your message on a wider scale.

Wherever you are on the book-writing journey, our five-pathway process will meet you there. We walk with you step-by-step, from getting the book written—choosing your ideal reader, picking the best topic, outlining your material, and even finding professionals to help you—all the way through to publishing, launching, and keeping sales going.

JOIN HERE: WWW.HAYHOUSE.COM/APMEMBERSHIP

Let us show you how a book can help you reach your goals—no matter what type of business you're growing!

HAY HOUSE